READING TO GROW

READING TO GROW

A FIELD GUIDE TO THE BIBLE

BERNARD JAMES MAUSER

WIPF & STOCK · Eugene, Oregon

READING TO GROW
A Field Guide to the Bible

Copyright © 2017 Bernard James Mauser. All rights reserved. Except for brief quotations in critical publications or reviews, no part of this book may be reproduced in any manner without prior written permission from the publisher. Write: Permissions, Wipf and Stock Publishers, 199 W. 8th Ave., Suite 3, Eugene, OR 97401.

Wipf & Stock
An Imprint of Wipf and Stock Publishers
199 W. 8th Ave., Suite 3
Eugene, OR 97401

www.wipfandstock.com

PAPERBACK ISBN: 978-1-5326-1614-3
HARDCOVER ISBN: 978-1-5326-1616-7
EBOOK ISBN: 978-1-5326-1615-0

Manufactured in the U.S.A.   APRIL 7, 2017

Dedication

This book is dedicated to Thomas Howe, Jim Marunowski, and my children (Isaiah, Levi, Justus, Corban, and Aletheia). Thomas A. Howe taught me how to dig deep to plumb the beautiful treasures of Scripture. James M. Marunowski demonstrated for our family a living faith and a dedication to God's word. My children are always on my heart. They are the next generation of Christians I'm responsible to train. It is my hope that my children and others are moved to know and love God more deeply as a result of this work.

CONTENTS

Preface | viii

Acknowledgments | xi

1. Hazardous Contents | 1
2. Athletics and the Bible: The Challenge of Understanding | 8
3. Lost in Translations? | 13
4. The Basics of Biblical Interpretation | 28
5. How Does Genre Help Us Understand? | 35
6. How Does Language Relate to God? | 48
7. Avoiding Land Mines in Interpretation | 57
8. Love Story From the Battlefield: Biblical Application | 65
9. Putting on the Bulletproof Vest: The Inerrancy Debate | 78

   Appendix   Guidelines for Bible Study | 93

   Bibliography | 95

Preface

IF JESUS HAD ONE hour to explain the most important aspects of dealing with and interpreting the Bible, what would he say? This book is an attempt at an answer to this question. I suspect Jesus would give answers to the big questions every Christian has about the Bible. His treatment would probably not be limited to the keys in observing, interpreting, and applying Scripture. He'd also most likely deal with ways to approach Bible difficulties and discuss different translations. Beyond this, one can argue that just as he did while teaching his disciples, and like his brother James, Jesus would provide motivation from Scripture to not only be hearers of the word, but people that live out the faith.

Having mentored and taught thousands of Christians in churches, seminaries, and universities, I've decided to create a short resource that explains the basics of dealing with the Bible. Just like soldiers have a field manual for the military that gives the essentials for what a warrior needs to know, this work also touches on what every Christian should understand and do in order to flourish.

Neil Postman has argued in *Amusing Ourselves to Death* that the influence of media has changed the way people learn and think. A program on television has a couple seconds to capture a person's attention or it's on to the next channel. This is also an age of social media where 30-second sound bites and 140 characters are the norm for how information is processed. Because these things have shortened our attention span, this book will provide a quick overview of how to interact with the Bible and questions about it.

Preface

You will find the book is written for the Christian who desires to move from being fed by others to feeding himself. One may say this book is elementary in that it touches on the basics of a wide number of issues. What this does not mean is that all the material is easy to grasp (though most of it certainly is). For example, the chapter titled "How Does Language Relate to God?" is a little more difficult due to the subject matter. It is my firm belief that a study of the more difficult chapters will yield the great fruit of a better understanding of God, His Word, and His world. Yet even if these more difficult chapters are not mastered, readers can consider themselves to be educated about what every good pastor wishes their congregation knew about handling Scripture.

Even a casual reading of this work exposes the reader to some of Christianity's leading thinkers throughout the ages in answering the basic questions. One must recognize that living in an information-rich age is exciting in that we can stand on the shoulders of theological giants to help us with new insights into Scripture. The resources of some of these sages are packed into the footnotes. One piece of advice given to me as a doctoral student was that the difference between a normal reader and one that is advanced is that the latter reads the resources in the footnotes. In the pages that follow, readers may find the motivation to dig deeper into these resources to build a more comprehensive knowledge of God's word.

Finally, this book is a result of the overflow of the love of God. The realization that God loves me despite my great sin caused a transformation. In turn, my love for God has driven me to discover the principles that help me know Him better through the Scriptures. God has clearly revealed how mankind ought to live. My love for others—starting with my own children—has compelled me to put these truths into this work so they too will know the Lover of their souls and how to live for Him. May the truths revealed in these pages galvanize all to offer themselves as living sacrifices to God with transformed hearts and minds. My hope is that this is not only a field guide for navigating subjects about Scripture, but that people will dive deeply into the living word to truly grow.

Acknowledgments

I AM INDEBTED TO many people for ideas and principles laid out in this book. It's been my pleasure and honor to have studied under Norman Geisler, Thomas Howe, Max Herrera, and Walter Kaiser. Their contributions to my understanding of God and this world are inestimable. I've shared many of the insights about the Bible taken from the works and words of these men for this book—and I highly recommend their books (see the footnotes and the bibliography).

I am also thankful to the many people who have read through this work and suggested improvements in the content. Among those who provided great feedback are Thomas Howe, Norman Geisler, Robert Evans, Ken Williams, Kristen Zuccola, Dave Sterrett, Elaine Linden, and my beloved wife Amber Mauser.

I'd also like to thank my cherished children Isaiah, Levi, Justus, Corban, and Aletheia for your patience and love. May you take to heart the truth that all Scripture is God-breathed and will equip you for every good work.

1

HAZARDOUS CONTENTS

"Man does not live on bread alone, but on every word from the mouth of God."

—JESUS (MATT 4:4)

THE BOOK YOU ARE now holding is extremely dangerous. Every year hundreds of thousands of Christians are being persecuted and martyred for their faith. As this book is designed to equip people to understand the Bible, there will be many that will do everything in their power to keep you from reading the forthcoming pages. In the big picture, you'll learn how to understand our origins, the meaning of life, the battle we are in (whether we know it or not), and our destiny. In nine short chapters you'll glean practical tips for understanding the Bible, answering Bible difficulties, choosing the best translation, and strategies for flourishing God's way. As a result, this work will prepare you to deploy the equipment necessary to face the darkest times, even when under attack from the greatest foes. I guarantee that if you take the time to study and apply the truths that you'll find in this book, you'll have the essential tools you need to thrive in the midst of perilous circumstances.

Three villains oppose us daily—the world, the flesh, and the devil. Those from the world of men often come in sheep's clothing. These are false teachers and teachings that call for a measure of discernment and judgment to oppose. There is also a spiritual battle occurring. Forces of darkness in the spiritual realm are invested in this battle. These evil forces' sole desire is the deception, death, and destruction of all of mankind. In order to combat this enemy, we will explore strategies to advance against the gates of hell, and win those that are captives to their deceit. The attack from within arises from our fallen propensities evoking apathy, ignorance, and pride. The apathy often comes from what we think will be momentary delays "until we have more time to really get into God's word." Our ignorance and pride are on display when thinking, "We need no one to teach us what the Bible means." We are removed from the Bible's context by factors like history, language, and culture. These factors do not need to be considered alone. This book equips you to valiantly overcome and heed our General's instruction.

Some may object to the characterization of warfare I've described. Yet this is exactly what every person faces. This book will equip you to use one of the most powerful weapons we have against our enemies—the word of God! D. L. Moody warns those who think the battle is over upon becoming a Christian.

> But a good many Christian people make this mistake: they think the battle already fought and won. They have an idea that all they have to do is put the oars down in the bottom of the boat, and the current will drift them into the ocean of God's eternal love. But we have to cross the current. We have to learn how to watch and fight, and how to overcome. The battle is only just commenced. The Christian life is a conflict and a warfare, and the quicker we find it out the better.[1]

The Christian should immediately realize that he is on the front lines of warfare upon conversion and seek to utilize the tools God has given him to succeed.

---

1. Moody, *Overcoming Life*, 9.

HAZARDOUS CONTENTS

Even beyond equipping us for the most important things we need in this life, the greatest significance of the Bible is it claims to be God's revelation of Himself. Understanding its message is the important task undertaken each time we read God's word. Knowing God's message tells us both how we ought to live and who He is. Christian theologian Bernard Ramm insightfully writes, "There is no profit to us if God has spoken and we do not know what He has said. Therefore it is our responsibility to determine the meaning of what God has given to us in Sacred Scripture."[2]

REVEALING PURPOSE AND MEANING

There are few of us who don't love a good joke. Consider the church sign: "Don't let worries kill you—let the church help." As funny as the sign was, if I missed the ambiguity inherent in the phrase it wouldn't be funny. Tied up with the enjoyment that comes in those hilarious moments when we grasp incongruity, we find ourselves in the midst of both transcendence and meaning. It is little wonder then why so many are addicted to comedies. Comedies help briefly appease an appetite hungering for meaning, purpose, and transcendence. Those who have read the Bible realize there is something far greater that it offers. What it promises is not a mere temporary satisfaction. The Bible offers hope for a person to be fully satiated and never again hunger or thirst for more (John 6:35).

In a world that is plagued with trying to find meaning and purpose, the Bible offers guidance in these areas that is clear and imbued with significance. The questions that are nearest to the heart deal with these very issues. The ancient philosophers recognized the natural desire of man for purpose. For those who take seriously the claim that the Bible is the word of God, it behooves us to explore what it says about matters that relate to meaning and those things we so eagerly desire.

The Bible has tremendous value as God reveals things with which our hearts resonate. The Word provides a context that

---

2. Ramm, *Protestant Biblical Interpretation*, 2.

situates us in a larger story and reveals a transcendent perspective to have meaning in life. The Scriptures offer the guidance along the path that promises true life.

In short, each person longs to reach God, and the means to do so is revealed most clearly in Scripture. What some pagans discovered about God's existence, through struggle, is evident even to children through what is called the perspicuity of Scripture. Perspicuity simply means that people can easily access the ideas in the Bible that are most important. The greatest thoughts in Scripture are those that explain God and the way we reach Him.

THE GUIDANCE OF WORLDVIEW

There are many useful things a person may need to know when seeking direction in life. A person may struggle with questions ranging from the trivial to those that will forever impact them. The question about whether one should wear a certain color socks, have corn flakes or eggs for breakfast, or even which amazing book on how to understand the Bible to read may be among those trivial questions. However, some questions are more important—like how can a person get to heaven? People need a way of seeing the world to help them live, which is provided in Scripture (this is called a biblical worldview).[3]

In many ways the Bible is like a map. Consider some advantages to having the tools necessary to read the map. It helps each individual steer a clear course. It also posts warning signs similar to what the old maps warned—that in certain areas of life *there be dragons*! Many of us, even those that know better, need the continual reminder that the warning is intended to help us and not to harm. There are concrete things we can avoid to stay out of trouble.

---

3. For the best book I have found that unpacks the many ways the Christian worldview affects all of life, read Nancy R. Pearcey's books *Total Truth* and *Saving Leonardo*. For a survey of different worldviews, James Sire has written the classic *The Universe Next Door*. For the best series of books in answering common slogans against Christians, read the many books written by Paul Copan on this subject.

HAZARDOUS CONTENTS

We can thus avoid the error of our ancestors (in a garden) in calling "good" what God has said is evil. The road map is significant in what it identifies as good, the principles that guide us, and how to be fruitful and holy in our endeavors. Considering the author of the map is also the author of history and nature, a person ignores what is written at his or her own peril.

The Bible also explains how there are unseen evils that can affect us. Scripture informs us that we are in a battle. Our greatest foes are spiritual forces of darkness. Apart from Scripture, we'd have little hope in knowing how to fight against such enemies. Charles Spurgeon, known as the Prince of Preachers, spells out the practical consequences of seeing this battle against Satan for what it is.

> Also, let it be remembered that, incidentally, the temptations of Satan are of service to the people of God. Fenelon said that they are the file that rubs off much of the rust of self-confidence. I may add, they are the horrible sound in the sentinel's ear, which is sure to keep him awake. One theologian remarked that there is no temptation in the world that is so bad as not being tempted at all, for to be tempted will tend to keep us awake. Whereas being without temptation, flesh and blood are weak. Though the spirit may be willing, yet we may be found falling into slumber. Children do not run away from their father's side when big dogs bark at them. The howlings of the Devil may tend to drive us nearer to Christ, may teach us our own weakness, may keep us upon our own watchtower, and may be the means of preservation from other ills. "Be sober, be vigilant; because your adversary the devil, as a roaring lion, walketh about, seeking whom he may devour." (1 Pet 5:8)[4]

---

4. Spurgeon, *Spurgeon on Prayer and Spiritual Warfare*, 500–501.

Reading to Grow

GLEANING WISDOM FROM THOSE THAT HAVE GONE BEFORE

It is said that youth is wasted on the young. Perhaps the sentiment of those who feel this way lament the way that they squandered their youth. It is easy to look back on life and wonder how different things might have been if you had known then what you know now. The instruction from the Bible, when it is properly understood, provides wisdom to the old and young so that all can avoid the mistakes that often come from bad decisions. We may also consider the wisdom of those in our midst as to their reflections on why we should read the Bible.

Every Christian tradition emphasizes the importance of reading and understanding the Bible. For the Eastern Orthodox: "All that is necessary for this world and the people in it —the Lord has stated in the Bible."[5] The Roman Catholic catechism says it "forcefully and specifically exhorts all the Christian faithful . . . to learn the 'surpassing knowledge of Jesus Christ,' by frequent reading of the divine Scriptures."[6] One Protestant confession, the Westminster Shorter Catechism, states:

1. **What is the chief end of man?**
   A. Man's chief end is to glorify God, and to enjoy him forever.

2. **What rule hath God given to direct us how we may glorify and enjoy him?**
   A. The Word of God, which is contained in the Scriptures of the Old and New Testaments, is the only rule to direct us how we may glorify and enjoy him.

3. **What do the Scriptures principally teach?**

---

5. Archimandrite Justin Popovich of Blessed Memory, "Can You Tell me How to Read the Bible and Why?" *Holy Scripture In The Orthodox Church.* Compiled by Father Demetrios Serfes, August 20, 2000. http://www.serfes.org/orthodox/scripturesinthechurch.htm.

6. *Catechism of the Catholic Church*, article 3.5, "Sacred Scripture in the Life of the Church. http://www.vatican.va/archive/ENG0015/__PS.HTM.

HAZARDOUS CONTENTS

A. The Scriptures principally teach what man is to believe concerning God, and what duty God requires of man.[7]

We can see in this sampling that all the major Christian traditions (Eastern Orthodox, Roman Catholic, and Protestant) emphasize the importance of knowing Scripture.

Although what is immediately evident is that the young need guidance, what should be clear to those of us who are older is that we too require divine guidance. One doesn't have to raise children to recognize how much guidance is necessary due to their undeveloped intellect and wisdom. We must consider that there is a far greater gap between us and God than there is between us and children. As children need those wiser to guide them in order to secure what is best for them, so too should we admit that God's counsel where He offers it in the Bible is to secure what is best for us. We should know what He has said. This book offers some of the tools necessary to attain this goal.

In sum, there are several reasons for why we should read the Bible. These include:

1. The Bible is a message from the Creator of the universe about Himself and how to live. This first point contains the fact that we can glean wisdom from the omniscient Creator about living and the divine "road map."
2. The Bible helps us find our place in a greater story, which acts as an aid to discover the purpose to our life.

With very little reflection each of us can resonate with Augustine's sentiment about our need for God. "You move us to delight in praising You; for You have formed us for Yourself, and *our hearts are restless* till they find rest in You."[8]

---

[7]. *Westminster Shorter Catechism*, assembly at Edinburgh, July 28, 1648. Sess. 19, questions 1–3. http://www.epcew.org.uk/wsc/WSC.html.

[8]. Augustine, *Confessions*, book 1.

2

ATHLETICS AND THE BIBLE
THE CHALLENGE OF UNDERSTANDING

MANY AMONG US LOVE sports. You'll find those that like to participate, some to watch, and others that enjoy both. There is something gripping about watching people compete and perform well. Most also recognize the labor that goes into training. It is not always easy, and often there is struggle or pain associated with exercise. Many have the suppressed lament, "I'd probably exercise more if only it didn't hurt." There is a parallel to studying the Bible that can be drawn here.

Think about the barriers of language, time, and culture that separate us from the text. These have the potential to keep us from biblical understanding. Those that are less identifiable come under what are called assumptions (or presuppositions). Digging into these areas can be painful, but one can reap a great reward with the proper discipline. One sees something similar in athletic training.

There are two goals of this chapter. First, we will look at the main barriers to understanding Scripture. Second, together we can glean some insights that should encourage us all to continue studying God's word.

THE STRUGGLE

The first obstacle to address is language. Most of us are not native speakers of Hebrew and Greek. Even if we are, there are differences between the modern spoken languages and the biblical languages. Few of us have studied the languages in which the Bible is written. It doesn't take much imagination to see how this can hinder us from knowing what is happening in the text.

Despite the problems that may potentially come from not knowing the original language, the meaning expressed in the original language may still be communicated to us today. The reason for this is while the language may be culturally relative, the meaning is not. A language can be created by a particular group or a person. For example, J. R. R. Tolkien created several languages to be used by the elves in his *Lord of the Rings* series. The meaning of what the elves said to each other could be communicated in different languages (despite symbols used as letters that may be different between them). This is because the meaning of what is said transcends languages. The language is material, the meaning is immaterial. For example, the following sentences have the same meaning even though the languages are different:

El perro es negro. (Spanish)

The dog is black.

In another example, this biblical text says, "In the beginning," from the opening of Genesis:

בְּרֵאשִׁית (Hebrew)

En el principio (Spanish)

ἐν ἀρχῇ (Greek)

All these examples illustrate that translation is not only possible, but undeniable.

Besides being undeniable, those denying the possibility of understanding between languages confuse words and terms. In logic, there is a distinction made between words, terms, and concepts. The two ends of the spectrum are words and concepts, and the term acts like a bridge between the two. You can sense the words on this page in different ways (hearing, sight, touch). Words are physical.

The concept is an idea—something not perceived by the senses but grasped immaterially in the mind. Concepts are completely subjective (accessible only to the subject). Terms are the carriers of meaning to individuals. The term is publicly accessible insofar as everyone can access the meaning of words. The meaning is more than the physical arrangement of letters themselves. Peter Kreeft writes,

> A term is the most simple and basic unit of meaning. A term is simply any word or group of words that denotes an object of thought.... A term is whatever can be used as the subject or predicate of a proposition. "Apple" has the same meaning whether it is in the proposition "Apples are fruits" or whether it is outside the proposition and merely "apple."[1]

The term may be more or less clearly understood as the main carrier of meaning. This is why a good definition can help us understand the meaning of a term that is unclear.

Undoubtedly, those who don't know the original language are dependent on others to properly communicate the meaning. Regardless, it doesn't entail that the meaning is impossible to access.

Language may be easy to overcome, but what about time and culture? We are separated from biblical events and people by thousands of years. One must consider the tools of the historian and the archeologist. Those in these fields put us in touch with many discoveries, unveiling valuable information that provides background and helps our understanding. With easy internet access, a person can glean an enormous amount of data about the history Scripture records. Knowing the circumstances of what is written brings clarity to historical-cultural concerns. For example, some have mistakenly read the condemnation of the church at Laodicea for being neither hot nor cold as saying God would rather you be completely turned off to him rather than on the fence (or lukewarm). Archeological discovery has revealed that Laodicea tried to bring in water from hot and cold springs from outside the city (the rancid lukewarm water arriving in the city made the people

---

1. Kreeft, *Socratic Logic*, 41.

who would drink it sick). People would travel to the hot springs for healing and the cold springs for refreshment. The condemnation to the church was, therefore, against the church neither providing healing nor refreshment. It had nothing to do with God preferring people to be completely turned off to him (as they are sitting on the fence of a decision).

Regardless of the distance in culture and time, there is always some similarity between us and those in Scripture. Admittedly, there may be nuances that are missed due to the gaps between us. However, we find commonality in many areas. All have the human struggle against the world, the flesh, and the devil. All have rebelled against God. All seek a purpose in life. All need restoration, along with guidance as to how to live and love.

The fourth area that keeps us from understanding revolves around assumptions brought to the text. These assumptions go by different names in books on this subject. They are identified as preunderstanding, presuppositions, preconceptions, or even worldview. These can be either accurately formed or not. If a person actually validates that his assumptions or worldview is correct, then when these are brought to the text to aid in interpretation it will bear good fruit (i.e., there will be proper understanding). When these are incorrect, then the fruit will be bad (i.e., there will be misunderstanding). This is the lesson Jesus teaches in Matt 7 and 12. We identify false teachers by the words they speak as they are inaccurate. We learn from the overflow of their heart their mouth speaks. Also, it is by their words they will be justified or condemned. Thus, it is our burden to make sure our assumptions are true. Yet, if they are, we can have confidence in proceeding to understand the text (ensuring we have taken into account the other factors previously mentioned).

There is one last note of encouragement that must not be overlooked about the areas just treated. This book is designed to begin to help people grasp the context of what is written in Scripture. In the chapters of this book, different devices that bridge the gap between us and the original audience are examined. One can then at least find an entry point to explore the history, time, culture, and assumptions of the original audience. The meaning of what God has communicated is within our grasp.

THE GOOD NEWS

One may still feel some angst about all the barriers that get in the way of understanding the Bible. I've suggested some of the ways these can be overcome, but there is even more hope for a beginner who wants immediate understanding. Here is the good news about understanding the Bible. The major things that people need to know about God, salvation, and how to live, are so accessible that a child can understand them. This is not to overlook the fact that the Bible is so rich that the greatest scholar can spend his life plumbing its depths. Instead, what needs emphasized is the doctrine of the perspicuity of Scripture. This doctrine says the main and the plain things are evident. This is why children can know all the things they ought to do and trust in the one true God for salvation.

There are two major reasons for this. The first is that Scripture reveals truths God wants to share with mankind. As revelation from God, the majority of what the Bible communicates expresses universal truths applicable to all humanity. God uses the language of Scripture to communicate to those of us in His creation. The second is a fact about the way God created us. All people on earth are created in God's image and share a common nature. As such, we have an intellect that can understand what is said. Not only that, but we experience the human condition together and recognize how the verities found in God's word speak to our deepest needs and teach us about Him.

Thus, the hope for understanding cannot be obscured by the aforementioned barriers. In fact, we are designed by our very nature to know. The knowing we experience when encountering the Scripture becomes one with us. It is meant to affect not only the mind, but also the heart. Our goal must be to allow God to reach us in this way, remembering the greatest command: to love the Lord our God with all our heart, soul, strength, and mind (Luke 10:27).

3

LOST IN TRANSLATIONS?

Fr. Robert Sirico, an American, recounts a time of studying in England. While visiting a restaurant with an incredible level of service, he felt compelled to offer the woman waiting on them a compliment: "Miss, you are a real pro!" The waitress and all the patrons who had heard this seemed taken aback. The priest asked a friend what was wrong and discovered that in England a pro is a prostitute.[1] This is a clear example of a misunderstanding that occurred, even though there was a common language. Even more of a challenge presents itself when translation is involved.

This chapter gives a rough overview of the major translations of the Bible. In the first section, we will examine the approaches to translating the original text (along with some examples of each). The second section explains the basics of textual criticism. The third briefly suggests some practical advice for choosing a translation.

WHAT'S IN A TRANSLATION?

Imagine watching a football game on television, and there are only seconds left. The team with the ball only has one opportunity to

---

1. Sirico, *Defending the Free Market*, 26–27.

score in order to win. The final play comes down to whether the receiver who had caught the pass landed in-bounds. The ability to determine where the receiver's feet landed could be affected depending on whether you were watching a television that was black-and-white or color. It's easier for you to discover the truth about what happened when seeing in color due to the clarity and contrasts in the picture.

Something similar is experienced when reading the Bible in the original language versus reading a translation. Reading the words of God in the original language allows you to see nuances not always picked up in a translation. How much we glean from the original is dependent upon the translation chosen. We can, however, still understand the major things going on in the text in many translations, much like watching a football game in black-and-white. Following the analogy, reading the original language would reveal what is going on in color. We find color breaking through our translation when it accurately transmits the meaning of the original language.

There are different approaches to translating the Bible into English. We can observe strengths and weaknesses in each. Knowing the differences can help in deciding which translation is best for you. All of these try to communicate the meaning in the original text, but *how* they do so leads to the differences.

Hebrew and Greek are inflected languages, while English is not. Practically speaking, what this means is that word order is less significant to determine the meaning of what is going on in these other languages. In English, word order is important. "Eve kisses Adam" is not "Adam kisses Eve." Inflected languages do not depend as much on word order to convey meaning. Instead, there is something about the words themselves that indicate their role – not necessarily the word order. For example, there is no difference in the meaning of the following Greek sentences (taken from 1 John 4:8) even though there is a difference in the word order:

1. *ho Theos agape estin*
2. *agape estin ho Theos*

In these, the translation to English remains "God is love."

The first approach to translation is called the "essentially literal" or formal equivalence. The formal equivalence tries to use the same words in the same order as in the original. When possible, the translator brings over the original language word-for-word into English without violating the syntax (or normal arrangement of words) of the English language. When possible, even the original structure is used. This occasionally leads to some odd phrases. Translations using a formal equivalence are the New King James Version (NKJV), Revised Standard Version (RSV), English Standard Version (ESV), and the New American Standard Bible (NASB).

A second popular approach follows what is called the dynamic or functional equivalence translation. This way of translating brings over what is expressed in the original text using a thought-for-thought equivalent meaning. The goal is for readers to grasp concepts of the text said in a familiar way. These are commonly used to introduce new believers and young Christians to God's word. Current examples of this approach are the New Living Translation (NLT), Contemporary English Version (CEV), and the Good News Bible (GNB).

An easy way to illustrate the difference between these two approaches is taken from 1 Kgs 2:10. A formal rendering says, "So David slept with his fathers and was buried in the city of David" (NASB). The dynamic equivalence says, "So David died and was buried in the city of David" (NLT). The NASB uses identical words as the original (in unusual English). The NLT captures the phrase "slept with his fathers" with the word "died." David's death "is expressed in a way that modern speakers would use to express the same idea today."[2]

A third approach mixes the formal and dynamic equivalence. This is sometimes called the mediating approach. Examples of this hybrid or mediating approach are the New International Version (NIV), Today's New International Version (TNIV), and the New Revised Standard Version (NRSV).[3]

---

2. Grudem and Thacker, *Why Is My Choice of A Bible*, 10.

3. There is a debate about some modern translations and their use of

Another important consideration to be aware of is that some of the more modern translations (like the TNIV and NRSV) use gender-inclusive language. Those responsible for this change in language try to make the text more in line with what they perceive to be modern preferences. For example, the translators of the NRSV wanted to be more inclusive in its language than the Revised Standard Version (RSV). Ron Rhodes notes five significant changes between the RSV and NRSV.

1. The word *father* occurs 601 fewer times in the NRSV than in the RSV.
2. The word *son* occurs 181 fewer times.
3. The word *brother* occurs 71 fewer times.
4. The words *he, him,* and *his* are either dropped or changed to *you, we,* or *they* over 3,400 times.
5. The word *man* is changed to human, mortal, or mortals over 300 times.[4]

Beyond the problems with altering what the text has said, some of these changes significantly affect whether one recognizes messianic prophecies. For example, consider Ps 34:20 in the RSV: "He keeps all his bones; not one of them is broken." In the NRSV it says, "He keeps all their bones; not one of them will be broken." The messianic prediction is lost due to the gender-inclusive change. While some of the changes in the text may help people understand that all people are included as representative of men, the alteration of verses like this on a grand scale takes away a person's ability to decide what is specific to man and what is general, as the decision is made for him in the translation process.

It goes without saying that differences between the approaches are significant for interpretation. Contrast, for example, the following translations of Matt 5:1–2:

---

gender-inclusive language. This is a good debate to know. Ron Rhodes has an excellent survey of the different issues in *The Complete Guide to Bible Translations*.

4. Rhodes, *Complete Guide to Bible Translations*, 50–51.

LOST IN TRANSLATIONS?

New American Standard Bible	New International Version
When Jesus saw the crowds, He went up on the mountain; and after He sat down, His disciples came to Him. He opened His mouth and *began* to teach them, saying . . .	Now when Jesus saw the crowds, he went up on a mountainside and sat down. His disciples came to him, and he began to teach them.

Notice the difference between the varied versions. The italics, which differ, indicate a word that is not in the original text, but one inferred from the context. Although the meaning of the two appears the same, note the omission. The NIV leaves out that Jesus opened his mouth.[5] Of course if he spoke, his mouth was opened. Can more be going on here?

Those using the formal equivalence may have kept the word "mouth" in the translation for a good reason. This detail about the word mouth links chapters 4 and 5 of Matthew. In Matt 4, Jesus is in the wilderness and tempted by Satan. We find in the initial rebuke of Satan, Jesus says, "It is written, 'Man shall not live on bread alone, but on every word that proceeds out of the mouth of God'" (Matt 4:4). The reader can connect the "mouth of God" that Jesus speaks of in chapter 4 with "opening His mouth" in chapter 5. This is another way the text is telling you that these words Jesus speaks in the Sermon on the Mount are the words of God—words on which to live.

A fourth approach is a paraphrase of the original. A paraphrase attempts to transmit the general idea being expressed using different words than are in the original. The purpose of this is to

---

5. "The Greek idiom uses two phrases, *anoigo to stoma* ('open the mouth') and *didasko* ('teach'), to express a single action. For the Greek reader opening the mouth and teaching were not two consecutive actions, but one act of speaking (see Acts 8:35, 10:34; Rev 13:6). The functional equivalent versions (NIV, TNIV, and NCV) recognize this idiom and so accurately render the Greek, 'he began to teach them.' The more literal NKJV and ESV are understandable, but they miss the Greek idiom and so introduce an unnatural English expression." Fee and Strauss, *How to Choose a Translation for All Its Worth*, 27.

make the meaning very accessible, to evoke in the paraphrase feelings similar to what a first century audience felt, and to help people who struggle to understand.[6] One popular paraphrase that does this is Eugene Peterson's book called *The Message*.[7] A paraphrase is good *when it accurately captures and transmits the meaning of the original text*. Today the popular paraphrases are The Message, J. B. Phillips New Testament, The Word on the Street, and The Living Bible.[8]

Here is a table that shares some of the different translations available today:[9]

Word-for-Word Formal Equivalence	Hybrid	Thought-for-Thought or Functional Equivalence	Paraphrase
Interlinear	TNIV	NAB	The Message
NASB	NIV	NLT	Phillips
AMP	NRSV	CEV	The Word on the Street
ESV		GNB	
NKJV		NCV	The Living Bible
RSV			
HCSB			

There is something important to remember about paraphrases. One can know whether something is a good paraphrase only if we know what is actually in the text. Consider this analogy: Suppose

---

6. Ibid., 33.

7. Fee and Strauss, 33. Fee and Strauss explain that Peterson views his work as an attempt at transculturation.

8. Grudem and Thacker, 12.

9. The abbreviations for the versions of the Bible are as follows: NASB is the New American Standard Bible. AMP is the Amplified Bible. ESV is the English Standard Version. NKJV is the New King James Version. RSV is the Revised Standard Version. HCSB is the Holman Christian Standard Bible. TNIV is Today's New International Version. NIV is the New International Version. NAB is the New American Bible. NLT is the New Living Translation. CEV is the Contemporary English Version. GNB is the Good News Bible. NCV is the New Century Version. NRSV is the New Revised Standard Version.

LOST IN TRANSLATIONS?

I described my mother as a gypsy from Vienna with one leg. How would you know whether my description is accurate? Recognize that the only way to judge the accuracy of my description is to know my mother in reality. This is similar to paraphrases about the word of God. Knowing God's Word allows you to gauge whether the paraphrase accurately captures what the text says. Examine these two passages side-by-side from The Message and the NIV.

New International Version 1 Cor 2:14–15	The Message 1 Cor 2:14–15
The person without the Spirit does not accept the things that come from the Spirit of God but considers them foolishness, and cannot understand them because they are discerned only through the Spirit. *The person with the Spirit makes judgments about all things*, but such a person is not subject to merely human judgments. (emphasis mine)	The unspiritual self, just as it is by nature, can't receive the gifts of God's Spirit. There's no capacity for them. They seem like so much silliness. Spirit can be known only by spirit—God's Spirit and our spirits in open communion. Spiritually alive, we have access to everything God's spirit is doing, and can't be judged by unspiritual critics.[A]

A. Peterson, *The Message/Remix*, 1671.

It appears the NIV seems to indicate the really spiritual person judges everything, while The Message does not.

Contrast another two passages from Matt 18:15–17.

New International Version	**The Message**
If your brother sins, go and point out their fault, just between the two of you. If they listen to you, you have won them over. But if they will not listen, take one or two others along, so that "every matter may be established by the testimony of two or three witnesses." If they still refuse to listen, tell it to the church; and if they refuse to listen even to the church, treat them as you would a pagan or a tax collector.	If a fellow believer hurts you, go and tell him—work it out between the two of you. If he listens, you've made a friend. If he won't listen, take one or two others along so that the presence of witnesses will keep things honest, and try again. If he still won't listen, tell the church. If he won't listen to the church, you'll have to start over from scratch, confront him with the need for repentance, and offer again God's forgiving love.[B]

B. Peterson, *The Message/Remix*, 1455.

These two texts say something different. It is easy when considering these texts to recognize the importance of knowing what is actually said (to judge for accuracy).

Pastor Gary Gilley suggests, "Paraphrases are not suitable for Bible study and have limited value for Bible reading."[10] This may seem harsh, but he doesn't say they have no value. One suggestion may be to avoid having a paraphrase as the primary source of feeding from God's word. Imagine that the only source of nutrition available to everyone was really tough steak. What if our teeth could only get stronger by chewing the steak, but that chewing it before they were strong was also painful? Suppose someone chewed it for you and offered you pieces for nutrition. Something similar can be said of the different approaches to translation. Of all the approaches, the paraphrase is the most chewed piece, and one may find what you are offered is not steak, but spoiled food without nutrition. Paul instructs in Heb 5:12–14 (NIV),

> For though by this time you ought to be teachers, you have need again for someone to teach you the elementary

10. Gilley, "I Just Wanted More Land," 70.

principles of the oracles of God, and you have come to need milk and not solid food. For everyone who partakes *only* of milk is not accustomed to the word of righteousness, for he is an infant. But solid food is for the mature, who because of practice have their senses trained to discern good and evil.

Understanding the meaning of the original text and discerning the basic teachings of Christianity is the solid food we should digest.

TEXTUAL CRITICISM

Due to the popularity of works that attack the reliability of the Bible, a Christian should understand how we can trust the Bible even with the claims of critics. Rest assured, the weight of evidence is in favor of the reliability of Scripture. Reliability is based on the number of manuscripts, when they were composed, and their accuracy. I'll briefly explain how biblical criticism is carried out and the actual implications of this process.[11]

One of the main purposes of textual criticism is to determine how reliable the message of a text is compared with the original message. The originals are called the autographs or the *autographa*. Early writings for ancient manuscripts are difficult to find due to the material they are written on. Ancient texts were written on papyrus, which comes from plants and vellum made of animal skins. These decompose due to their nature. The textual critic tries to discover the original message.

The resources a New Testament critic relies on include Greek manuscripts, ancient versions, places where Scripture is quoted in the church lectionaries, and citations in the correspondence of early church fathers. They get all these different sources together and see where one text agrees with another and where it doesn't. In every place where there is a disagreement between texts it is called a *variant*. The textual critic studies the difference between the different readings and tries to discover what the original said. If you

---

11. One good introduction to the study of textual criticism is David Alan Black's book *New Testament Textual Criticism: A Concise Guide.*

got a letter for the next four days and each was slightly different you'd have four variants.

1. You have won a new ca%. Please contact us to have it delivered.
2. You h@ve won a new car. Please contact us to have it delivered.
3. You have won a new car. Please conta%t us to have it delivered.
4. You have won a new car. Please contact us to have it de&ivered.

Note how you can easily discover the meaning of what the text is despite these four variants.

Common examples of variants New Testament scholars find are transposed word or letter order (metathesis), abbreviations, writing a letter or word once when it should have been written twice, or twice when it should have been written once (haplography or dittography), combining the last letter of the word with the following word (fusion), separating one word into two (fission), or confusing words that sound alike (homophony).[12] Abbreviations were common for special words like Jesus, Christ, Lord, and God. Known as *nomina sacra*, this shorthand recognized the sacredness of certain names, and they were used "to express reverence and devotion."[13] However, if one scribe writes the entire word and another the abbreviation, each counts as a variant. With an increased number of manuscripts you'll find an increased number of variants. A textual critic would add all the variants between the manuscripts and come up with what sounds to be a rather large number. However, one must pay attention to the kind of variants one is talking about and what the evidence really shows (especially considering the number of manuscripts we actually have for the Scriptures).

What are the number of manuscripts for the New Testament? Consider the following chart comparing the manuscripts with the best we have of other ancient texts:

---

12. Richards, *735 Baffling Bible Questions*, 9.
13. Kostenberger, Bock, and Chatraw, *Truth Matters*, 128.

LOST IN TRANSLATIONS?

ANCIENT TEXT	WHEN COMPOSED	EARLIEST COPY	TOTAL COPIES
Iliad	8th century BC	400 BC	643
Tacitus	100 AD	1100 AD	20
Gallic Wars, Caesar	100–44 BC	900 AD	10
New Testament	50–100 AD	114 AD	5,800 Greek 10,000 Latin 10,000–15,000 in Coptic, Syriac, Armenian, Georgian, etc. Total 25,000–30,000.

Note the gap between when each was composed and the earliest copy, as well as the total number of copies. It is wildly understated to say the textual evidence the New Testament has is superior to all other ancient documents.[14]

In addition to the manuscripts mentioned, there is also the writings of the early church fathers we can use to discover the New Testament. The church fathers, or patristics, wrote extensively about the meaning of different texts in the New Testament. One can reconstruct every single doctrinal tenet (e.g., virgin birth, substitutionary atonement, death, burial, resurrection of Jesus) of the Christian faith from these writings alone even if every Bible in existence was destroyed.[15]

---

14. There are several works that can guide a person to understand textual transmission and disputed passages. One great resource is Norman Geisler's *Systematic Theology: In One Volume*, where he deals with the Bible. Also, it is important to understand the difference between reliability of the Scripture and the inerrancy of the word of God. The first means that it can be trusted to say what was originally written. The second is that there can be no error in the Bible because God cannot error and it is his word. See the last chapter on inerrancy for more information.

15. J. Warner Wallace makes this point in *Cold Case Christianity*, as does one of the world's leading textual critics Daniel B. Wallace in Lee Strobel's *The*

Knowing this information, what can we make about claims from certain popular critics that there are between 200,000 and 400,000 variants? Considering there are so many manuscripts that you can place side by side, this is actually a surprisingly small number. As mentioned, the more copies you have the more variants you'll find. Mark Roberts uses the following mathematical example from a book by the critical scholar Bart Ehrman that points out this number:

> This book [by Bart Ehrman] has almost 50,000 words. Suppose I asked two people to make copies of the book by hand. Suppose, further, that they made one mistake every 1,000 words (99 percent accuracy). When they finished, each of their manuscripts would have 50 mistakes, for a total of 100. This doesn't sound too bad, does it? But suppose I asked 2,000 people to make copies of my book. And suppose they also made a mistake every 1,000 words. When they finished, the total of mistakes in their manuscripts would be 100,000. This sounds like a lot of variants—more than the words in my book. . . . But in fact the large number of variants is a simple product of the large number of manuscripts.[16]

One really should not lose sleep over discovering there are variants that scholars find in the biblical texts. Even radical biblical critics like Bart Ehrman say of these variants, "To be sure, of all the hundreds of thousands of textual changes [i.e., variants] found among our manuscripts, most of them are completely insignificant, immaterial, and of no real importance of anything other than showing the scribes could not spell or keep focused any better than the rest of us."[17]

So what do scholars find when they try to determine how reliable the Bible is? Sir Frederic Kenyon announces the verdict of the majority of scholars:

Case for the Real Jesus.
 16. Roberts, *Can We Trust the Gospels*, 33–34.
 17. Ehrman, *Misquoting Jesus*, 207.

The interval then between the dates of the original composition and the earliest extant evidence becomes so small as to be in fact negligible, and the last foundation for any doubt that the Scriptures have come down to us substantially as they were written has now been removed. Both that authenticity and the general integrity of the books of the New Testament may be regarded as finally established.[18]

One of the leading textual critics, the late Bruce Metzger, finds the New Testament 99.5 percent reliable, with only a few places where you can question the text.[19] John A. T. Robinson places the accuracy of the New Testament at 99.9 percent.[20] Remember that these variants are all due to copyist errors and do not affect the inerrancy of the original manuscripts.

What can be said of these small percentages? These numbers do *not* indicate that anything has been lost of the original text. The real question scholars have that include these small percentages is whether there is *extra* text in the Scripture. The main two passages that are debated among scholars as to whether they are in the original text are the story of the woman in John 8:1–11 and in Mark 16:9–20. The important point to realize is that the debate does not call into question whether these texts are true, but whether these particular texts were in the original. In the final assessment, the Bible is reliable and at worst we have 100 percent of the text with a little more added.

CHOOSING A TRANSLATION

The greatest scholars differ as to which approach to translation is superior. If they differ, how can we expect anyone to discover which is best? The easy answer to this question is that we must simply use our common sense as to the best strategy, while recognizing that newer translations will continue to come out.

18. Kenyon, *Bible and Archeology*, 288–29.
19. Metzger, *Chapters in the History*, 144–45.
20. Robinson, *Introduction to the Textual Criticism*, 14.

One thing you can do is use the many resources the internet provides. When studying, compare what several translations say. One translation may more accurately capture what the original says or lend greater clarity to what is going on in the passage. Both form-driven and meaning-driven translations strive to protect the message of Scripture. Form-driven translations emphasize the original structure; meaning-driven translations focus more on trying to communicate the meaning in an easily accessible way. David Dewey insightfully remarks, "The truth, however, is that we need both form-driven and meaning-driven translations. Wise Christians will equip themselves with at least one of each and compare them regularly."[21]

Some Bible versions may simply be easier to read than others. As the goal in communication is to unite one person's thoughts with another person, all should strive to have people read the Bible version that is easiest to understand.[22] Under the

---

21. Dewey, *User's Guide to Bible Translations*, 200.

22. The three main approaches each have a different goal in what they are trying to achieve in their translation. Understanding these differences may help you sort through which translation you'd prefer. In their book titled *How to Choose a Translation for All Its Worth* (34), biblical scholars Gordon D. Fee and Mark L. Strauss offer the following advice for your consideration:

Functional (dynamic) equivalence: alters the form until the text is natural.
Formal (literal) equivalence: alters the form until the text is comprehensible.
Mediating (taking elements of the two above): alters the form until the text is clear.

The differences between these three help us see what the scholars aim for in producing their version of the Bible.

In the first, the translators communicate the natural idioms of the Greek into common English. This is the most accessible of the three. The weakness in this approach is that there is much more interpretation involved in the translation and so some of the original meaning along with nuances in the text may be lost.

In the second, the original language is preserved along with the peculiar phrases. This gives the reader an opportunity to access the original text, but also makes it more difficult to understand. Though there is less interpretation going on here, it is difficult for people unfamiliar with the historical and biblical context.

In the third, there is an attempt to strike a balance between the two approaches. As a middle position, it shares the strengths and weaknesses of the other two. It is clearer than the formal approach, but also less natural than one that is fully

best circumstances this must be done without losing the original message.[23]

The reader should, therefore, use wisdom in selecting which translation to use. As the circumstances differ when selecting a translation, there is no one-size-fits-all translation to recommend. Studying God's word is one of the most important things we can do. Remember the words of Jesus to the Father: "Sanctify them by the truth; your word is truth"(John 17:17). A good Bible translation helps us access the truth and has the power to change your life because it is the word of God.

---

functional. It also has more interpretation than the formal, but tries to allow for greater comprehension for those unfamiliar with the original context. See also Rhodes, *Complete Guide to Bible Translations*, for more information.

23. All agree that the greatest dangers for losing that message happen in paraphrases.

4

THE BASICS OF BIBLICAL INTERPRETATION

Each person has spent countless hours before reading this book learning the art and science of interpretation. As a child you absorb thousands of details about the structure of language, vocabulary, culture, and figures of speech to help you understand what your parents say. This is all done without formal training. We don't have the same advantage with the biblical text, which is why we study to put ourselves in the position to better understand the text. The basic approach of all interpretation takes into consideration both grammar and history (known as the grammatical-historical context of a passage) to aid in understanding.

If a person ignores how to read the text properly, this is when the trouble starts. If people don't have the correct approach, even well-known biblical stories lose their significance. How many times has it been said that the problem when Peter tries to walk on water is he takes his eyes off of Jesus? Those saying this then go on to spend most of the time focusing on Peter (not Jesus)!

This chapter will focus on the principles of interpretation with the goal of understanding.

THE BASICS OF BIBLICAL INTERPRETATION

OBSERVATION

When a person begins to study the Bible, the first thing to do is simply to note what is evident about the text. Here are some questions you can ask to discover the details available in observation:

1. What is the type of literature or genre you are reading (e.g., epistle, gospel, wisdom, narrative, etc.)?
2. Who is the author?
3. What is the historical period in which the text is written?
4. What is the historical background of the events of the text?
5. Who is the audience addressed in the text?
6. What is the structure of the book (e.g., argumentative, chiastic, etc.)?
7. What do the names of the characters or places mean?
8. Are there parallel characters, whose relation is important for interpretation, that may be contrasted or compared in other parts of the text (e.g., Rahab and Achan; Saul and David)?
9. What words are repeated? Of those, which don't you know the meaning of?
10. What questions can you ask of each verse? Write these down as you read.

Your observations of the text can enrich your study as you research to answer to these questions. For example, some may be unaware of what a chiastic structure is (we explore this later). This would be good to look up in order to help you identify it in the biblical text. You'll note in the next step how there are other observations that can help you grasp the meaning of the text. Much of the labor of finding answers to observations can be diminished as people now have the ability to quickly look things up with the internet (e.g., finding the meaning of names is easy online).

Some elements are easy to find with a little research, but others require you to put some of your thoughts together differently than what is common to many of the Bible stories. The harder work that comes from studying the Bible can yield great fruit. Looking at parallels, for example, can reveal foreshadowing of one story in another or similar attributes between counterparts. Think of people in the Bible who were 1) forced to move to Egypt, 2) a ruler puts the promised one in danger, and 3) returned to the land to worship God. It immediately strikes me that these three things happen to Abraham, Israel, and Jesus.

HOW TO READ THE BIBLE

I remember starting seminary and taking my first Old Testament class. The professor said to write down the three most important principles of interpretation (which is known as hermeneutics). I waited eagerly and wrote down the following: "Context, context, context." After my brief chuckle, the professor explained the real importance of context in properly discovering the meaning of Scripture.

The context refers to all that surrounds a particular word that helps to clarify its meaning. A person does well to heed the advice of the title of the book, *Never Read a Bible Verse*.[1] This seems stunning in some ways. However, if you understand that the meaning of a given verse is made clear when that verse is in its context, then this maxim makes sense. Isolated verses ("there is no God") actually mean something quite different when looked at in context ("the fool says in his heart there is no God"). Even paragraphs can make greater sense when seen in light of the rest of the book in which they are written. Biblical books make more sense when looked at in the context of the entire Bible.

When beginning to study the Bible you can take notes on things that help you to get a handle on what the text is saying. Take an account of things you observed and note that the context includes understanding the following:

---

1. Koukl, *Never Read A Bible Verse*.

1. All your observations (including important and difficult terms in the text)
2. Possible figures of speech
3. How the text relates to the paragraph
4. How the paragraph relates to the book
5. How the book relates to the rest of the Bible
6. Ask what this verse may tell you about God
7. The structure of the book through an outline you make

In order to discover all of these things you may have to read the entire book (not just the part you are concerned about) several times. Often when you get a letter from someone, you read the whole thing. All too often people miss the context of particular verses because they fail to read the entire book. The following are some basic principles for understanding the Bible:

The text should be understood in its normal sense.

The default position when reading a text is to understand it literally. You read a passage and try to see whether it makes sense with what you know of reality to take this in a straightforward way. This doesn't mean you shouldn't recognize figures of speech (in reality, people use figures of speech all the time). We should *not* hold to a wooden-literal view (meaning there is no flexibility) in how we interpret Scripture. Consider what is obvious in how you understand, for example, that God owns "the cattle on a thousand hills" (Ps 50:10). What is this saying? If you think it means that God doesn't own the cattle on a thousand and one hills you hold a wooden-literal view of interpretation. If you think it means He owns all the cattle, you reject the wooden-literal view.

Another important point to note is the genre of the text you are reading. If the text is historical narrative (like Genesis, Exodus, and Acts), then this is a record of what happened (it is descriptive). Embedded in this there may be prescriptive elements (meaning it tells what you ought to do), but the prescriptive and descriptive are not the same. We will discuss more about genre in a later chapter.

The word of God is logical.

The presupposition we start with is that God cannot contradict himself. One Scripture cannot contradict another. This is sometimes referred to as the principle that "Scripture interprets Scripture." I don't prefer this, as humans are ultimately the ones interpreting both. Scripture isn't really interpreting anything, but what it is revealing cannot contradict other things it is revealing. When there is a tension between certain verses that appear to contradict, it is more than probable that you've misunderstood one or both of the verses. Truths from the text can be systematized to fit into a coherent worldview because Scripture is logical.

All the different types of language used in Scripture presuppose that there is a reality that is described.

The Bible uses parables, symbols, figures of speech, and allegories to communicate truths about reality to mankind. In many cases you'll need to understand how things relate to each other in order to take away the lesson. I provide a more detailed analysis of this in the chapter "How Does Language Relate to God."

Interpret personal experiences in light of Scripture, not vice versa.

Remember that the Bible can help you discern truth from error. If you have an experience that seems to contradict Scripture, then it is probable that you've misinterpreted Scripture, *or* you've misinterpreted your experience (or both). Judge your experience in light of Scripture and not Scripture in light of your experience.

The Scripture has one meaning, but it has many applications.

There are no secret meanings under the text (this has more to do with occultism or Gnosticism than interpretation). Our goal is to understand the meaning of the text. The text may be applied in a variety of ways, but there is one meaning. It is of greatest importance to first understand what the text means before trying to apply it. We will look more at application in the chapter devoted to that subject.

DEALING WITH BIBLE DIFFICULTIES

There are certainly some difficult passages in the Bible. You may wonder what a certain thing means, and that could be frustrating. However, I think more often than not we find ourselves in the same position that Mark Twain was in when he said, "It is not the things I don't understand in the Bible that bother me, it is the things I do understand that bother me."

There are more scholars who have dealt with difficult passages than I'd have time to detail. Gleason Archer, Lawrence Richards, R. A. Torrey, Norman Geisler, and Thomas Howe have all spent countless hours making sense of these difficulties. I'd recommend reading all of their resources (many are free online). Following Geisler and Howe's section from the general method for dealing with difficulties in *When Critics Ask*, here are some of the common ways to think about texts that are hard to grasp.

1. Realize that something you don't understand is not necessarily unexplainable.
2. Don't assume the Bible is guilty until proven innocent.
3. Don't confuse our interpretation with God's infallible revelation.
4. Understand difficult passages in light of clear ones.

5. Remember the Bible is not only 100 percent divine, it is also 100 percent human (genre matters).
6. Don't assume a partial or divergent account is false.
7. Don't demand New Testament citations of the Old Testament be exact quotes.
8. Don't assume the Bible approves of all it records (it records evil things it doesn't approve).
9. Don't forget the Bible uses the language of common people (we refer to the sunset even though it doesn't technically do this).
10. The Bible uses round numbers (so do we all the time).
11. Remember that only the original text is without error (not every copy).
12. Remember that later revelation supersedes previous revelation (God's nature doesn't change even if the way He deals with His people does).[2]

Ultimately, you will deal with a greater number of passages that are clear when studying the Bible than those that are unclear. Where you do encounter some that you aren't sure of, employ many of the tools available for Bible study. Realize that there are many resources available free online and use them. If you really want to grow in understanding God's word, keep studying your Bible. Don't confuse devotional reading with Bible study, as the two are *not* the same.

This chapter has touched upon basic principles of how to interpret your Bible. In the upcoming chapters there is more to learn that can build upon these principles. For a summary of these principles that you can copy and that will help you study the Bible, see "Guidelines for Bible Study" in the appendix at the end of the book.

---

2. Geisler and Howe, *When Critics Ask*, 15–27. More information on how to interpret difficulties found in the Bible here: http://defendinginerrancy.com/bible-difficulties/.

5

HOW DOES GENRE HELP US UNDERSTAND?

ONE OF MY SEMINARY professors was a master at using humor to enhance the lessons I learned. Along with his humor there was the occasional prank on the unsuspecting. Before the age of compact disks, many classes he taught were recorded on audio tapes. These would require him to stop after about forty-five minutes of recording, so the tape could be flipped over and he could continue. On more than one occasion students found themselves thinking they had missed something because he'd *begin* the recording with, "Third . . . " or "and that is the most important thing to learn in this class." Once students learned more about this professor, they'd realize his antics and understand what was really happening in the lectures. Understanding biblical genre does something similar for us in providing crucial information to help us understand the text when we often are confused about what is happening.

Before diving in to each type of genre, we should start with a definition. A genre simply refers to the literary category, form, or style of a text. A biblical text is to be understood in relation to its genre as part of the context in which it is written. Knowing the genre of what you are reading helps you understand what is said.[1] Thomas A. Howe, professor of Bible and biblical languages at Southern Evangelical Seminary, explains, "Genre classification enhances our understanding of meaning, or it may qualify our understanding of meaning, but genre does not determine meaning."[2]

This chapter will provide a survey of the major types of biblical genre and some suggestions on how best to discover the meaning of the text where these genres occur in Scripture. It is important to be aware that this chapter is a survey, and entire books have been written on each of these genres. I list some recommended books in the footnotes for additional understanding.[3] Each genre is not given in order of importance.

WISDOM LITERATURE

There is wisdom literature peppered throughout the Scripture. The major books classified as wisdom literature are Proverbs, Job, Ecclesiastes, and Song of Songs. There are also some psalms identified as such, like 1, 32, 34, 37, 49, 78, 111, 112, 119, 127, 128, and 133.[4] There are certain characteristics that mark wisdom literature. Walt Kaiser lists seven of them:

1. Alphabetic acrostics (successive verses begin with successive letters of the Hebrew alphabet)

2. Numerical sayings ("six things the Lord hates; yea, seven . . .")

---

1. Ryken, *How to Read the Bible as Literature*, 25
2. Howe, "Does Genre Determine Meaning?," 528.
3. Any person who has acquaintance with these books knows that the authors have differences in opinion regarding how to interpret certain Scriptures. Also, there are philosophical assumptions each person holds that causes the primary reasons for disagreement. One of the most destructive beliefs is that we can never reach the meaning of the text but are stuck in a hermeneutical spiral from which we can never emerge with the real meaning. The best refutation of this position is a book on the philosophy of hermeneutics by Thomas Howe, called *Objectivity in Biblical Interpretation*. This is not a book on "how to" interpret the Bible. It is a book on whether we can know the meaning of the Bible, and it persuasively answers in the affirmative.
4. Kaiser and Silva, *Introduction to Biblical Hermeneutics*, 99.

HOW DOES GENRE HELP US UNDERSTAND?

3. "Blessed" sayings
4. "Better" sayings ("better the little the righteous have than the wealth of many wicked")
5. Comparisons and admonitions
6. Addresses of father to son
7. The use of proverbs, similes, rhetorical questions, and phrases such as "listen to me"[5]

The other important aspect to know is how to interpret wisdom literature. You may encounter contradictory advice, like Prov 26:4–5: "Do not answer a fool according to his folly, or you yourself will be just like him. Answer a fool according to his folly, or he will be wise in his own eyes." The key principle to keep in mind is to look where this is found. As Proverbs is wisdom literature, you need wisdom to know when to answer a fool!

One can also see from this example that these Proverbs are general guidelines for living wisely. They are not universal principles, and they are *not* guarantees from God. Biblical scholars Gordon Fee and Douglas Stuart explain nine rules to understand the Proverbs:

1. Proverbs are often parabolic (i.e., figurative, pointing beyond themselves).
2. Proverbs are intensely practical, not theoretically theological.
3. Proverbs are worded to be memorable, not technically precise.
4. Proverbs are not designed to support selfish behavior—just the opposite!
5. Proverbs strongly reflecting ancient culture may need sensible "translation" so as not to lose their meaning.
6. Proverbs are not guarantees from God but poetic guidelines for good behavior.
7. Proverbs may use highly specific language, exaggeration, or any variety of literary techniques to make their point.

5. Ibid.

8. Proverbs give good advice for wise approaches to certain aspects of life but are not exhaustive in their coverage.

9. Wrongly used, proverbs may justify a crass, materialistic lifestyle. Rightly used, proverbs will provide practical advice for daily living.[6]

PROPHECY

Prophecy is a popular topic. Those familiar with the Bible can tell you there are four "major" prophetic books (Isaiah, Jeremiah, Ezekiel, and Daniel) along with twelve "minor" prophets (Amos, Habakkuk, Haggai, Hosea, Joel, Jonah, Malachi, Micah, Nahum, Obadiah, Zechariah, and Zephaniah). The reason they're called major and minor prophets is because of the length of what they've written and *not* their importance. Prophetic literature contains elements of both foretelling the future and forthtelling the truth of God's word. The prophets are identified as messengers of God and confirmed as such via miracles.

Prophecy acts as a divine fingerprint to help us identify the Messiah after his arrival. These were specific and unambiguous predictions (completely unlike modern "prophets" like Nostradamus). Two famous passages filled with messianic prophecies are found in Isa 53 and Ps 22. In these you find things as specific as dividing garments among them by casting lots, the messiah's heart bursting, bones dislocated, people mocking him saying let the Lord deliver him, and being silent before accusers, killed with criminals, and buried with the rich. We find in other prophets the city the Messiah would be born in (Bethlehem, Mic 5:2), and that he'd be betrayed by a friend (Judas, Ps 41) for thirty pieces of silver (not twenty-nine of gold), which would be thrown into the temple and used to buy a potter's field (Zech 11).

The important thing to understand is that some of what is predicted hundreds of years before it happened has already happened, and some of it has not. You'll have to study to see which

---

6. Fee and Stuart, *How to Read the Bible for All Its Worth*, 240–41.

of the prophecies have happened and which haven't. Even some prophecies of the Messiah—some of which have come to pass during the life of Jesus—haven't been completely fulfilled and will not be until his second coming. One should be aware that there is a huge debate among believers about what will still happen and what has already been fulfilled. All sides need to explore the arguments and the history of competing interpretations to help in discovering the truth. A Bible dictionary can quickly bring you up to speed regarding the history of each prophet.

Guidance for identifying a false prophet is given in a couple places. In Deut 18:22 we learn that if a prophet speaks in the Lord's name but his prediction doesn't come to pass he is not a true prophet. Also, suppose someone claims to be a prophet and what they say comes to pass *but* they say, "let's worship other gods." Deuteronomy 13:15 explains those are also false prophets. When these instructions were offered, the penalty was death for the prophet who does so in the nation of Israel (note the historical and cultural restrictions).

The most difficult thing in interpreting prophecy is understanding how there can be two fulfillments of the same prophecy—introducing what is called the alleged double sense of prophecy. It is important to know that even if there are two fulfillments (one close to the time it is made and another many years later) there is still one meaning that can be applied to both cases. For example, when Isaiah offered the sign of the virgin conceiving and giving birth to a son, this was initially for King Ahaz and Israel (Isa 7:14). It was later recognized as also being a sign to the followers of Jesus.

Some prophecies have both a near and a more distant fulfillment in view. Some have explained that it is best to think of prophecy not as mere prediction, but as achieving the complete plans of God. This helps people understand that a prophecy is not fulfilled until it is "filled full" with the entire purpose that God has for what is foretold.[7] As Kaiser explains, there are three aspects to prophecy:

1. The predicted word that preceded the event toward which it pointed.

---

7. Greidanus, *Modern Preacher and the Ancient Text*, 238.

2. The historical means by which God kept that predicted word alive for each succeeding generation, by giving what amounts to down payments that connected the first announcement of the word with its climatic fulfillment.

3. The ultimate fulfillment of that word in the New Testament era of the First Advent, or in the days of the Second Advent.[8]

PARABLES

Jesus often used parables to illustrate a point. They are fiction and figures of speech that worked to help share some truth. Jesus often shared truth using the device of a parable in order that those who truly cared sought the meaning behind the parable and grasped its truth. Those who didn't care to grasp the truth could pass by without concern. Another advantage of the parable is that its story was a memorable way to communicate a complex spiritual truth. In order to understand the parable you'd have to "break the code," in a manner of speaking, to see what is represented. Leland Ryken explains, "[Jesus] concealed the truth from immediate perception in order to reveal it to listeners who were willing to ponder his parables."[9]

There are real consequences to how you identify different people in the parables. Is, for example, the foolish *servant* of the master who goes on a long journey (in the parable of the talents in Matt 25) a believer or not? Most say no, as this servant is thrown into outer darkness where there is weeping and gnashing of teeth (Matt 25:30). After all, none will be crying in heaven. The question becomes, can a servant of the master be unfaithful, or are all those unfaithful servants unbelievers? A highly favored interpretation is that this foolish servant refers to unbelievers. Another reason for this is that weeping and gnashing of teeth occur in hell. This person is weeping and gnashing their teeth, therefore they are in hell.

However, what if not every reference to weeping and gnashing of teeth is a reference to hell? Suppose some occur when the

---

8. Kaiser and Silva, *Introduction to Biblical Hermeneutics*, 158.
9. Ryken, *How to Read the Bible as Literature*, 9.

master returns to give rewards to the faithful servants. On this interpretation, unfaithful servants are not invited to the banquet where rewards are given. One may say they didn't come properly dressed (clothed in good works perhaps)—just like the friend of the king who arrived at the wedding without proper clothes (Matt 22:11–14).

How would this latter interpretation handle the problem that there is no weeping or gnashing teeth in heaven, so this can't be the correct view? One response is that the rewards are given before (Rev 20:12) God wipes every tear from the eyes of believers (Rev 21:4). There are a number of parables that deal with this subject that one needs to study to "break the code" so that they can be understood properly.[10] The proper belief can help to motivate our proper action. We should make sure we are the faithful servant when the master returns and not the foolish one. This is just one example of the in-house debate among Christians as to how to interpret some parables (meaning you can be a Christian scholar and still disagree).

EPISTLE

The epistle is a letter. The letter has a structure of which the reader should be aware (especially important in long letters like Romans, Hebrews, and the letters to the Corinthians). This structure helps orient you to the topics the author addresses. It also makes the reader aware of the argument. The key advice when reading epistles is to realize they are supposed to be read and understood in their entirety. When you get a letter from a friend, you'll read the entire thing. It's a good practice to read the entire letter in a sitting over and over again to get a feel for what he is saying. Keep in mind when reading that you should think about what each verse is saying in the context of its paragraph (or as has been said, "think paragraphs").

---

10. Zane Hodges has an excellent book presenting one side of this discussion called *Grace In Eclipse: A Study of Eternal Rewards* that I think is worth reading. You'll also find Fee and Stuart as well as Kaiser and Silva discuss the parables in their books.

NARRATIVE

Narrative, or story, is the dominant form of literature in the Bible. This includes historical descriptions of events. Look for details when trying to understand Hebrew narrative. Observe as many elements of narrative as possible to help discover the point.

You should not only look to the characters in the story, but characteristics of all the things described (whether it is geographical location, people, or even the movements—pay attention for significance). You'll also want to note everything about the dialogue that takes place. If something is mentioned in God's word, there is an important reason it is there (even if not everything is equally important). It is our job to try to discover how the details of the text enhance our understanding about God or what He wants us to know. If someone alters something that has been said, this is significant.[11] For example, note the difference as to what God instructs about the tree of the knowledge of good and evil in the second chapter of Genesis versus what Eve says in the third. Eve adds to what God has said. One can also note that Adam is there too, so he could have been a leader, corrected her misstatement, or stopped her from eating the fruit.

We should also pay attention to plot and its narrator. The structure to look for is the beginning of the action, the generation of the conflict (and where it is most intense), the climax, the unraveling of conflict, the resolution of conflict, and where the action ends.[12] The plot is often narrated by people, but also by God. As all of Scripture is from God you'll see, as biblical scholar Sidney Greidanus notes, "the narrator is almost always omniscient."[13] As a result of this perspective we learn about God, His thoughts, and how He will deal with the people involved.

The common literary structures to look for are repetition, inclusion, and chiasm. If an author repeats something there is probably some significance to what is repeated. Repetition sometimes

---

11. Greidanus, *Modern Preacher and the Ancient Text*, 203.
12. Ibid., 203–5.
13. Ibid., 206.

reveals the structure of the text and helps you focus in on a central message to take away. Repetition may not only include words or phrases repeated, but also the root words used in various places in a text. For example, the ark that Noah builds is the same word as the ark that saves the young Moses from destruction by Pharaoh.[14]

Inclusion (or *inclusio*), Greidanus explains, is a type of repetition that "marks primarily the limits of a literary unit by repeating at the end words and phrases from the beginning."[15] This literary device places brackets around a text. An example of this is found in Jer 1:11 and 24:3 where God asks him, "What do you see, Jeremiah?" The most famous is probably Ps 8, which opens and closes with the inclusion "O Lord, our Lord, how majestic is your name in all the earth!" (Ps 8:1, 8:9). This structure points to parallels and acts like an envelope or book ends to encompass the text.

Chiasm, another type of repetition, may be the most difficult to find. Chiastic structures order verses, sentences, and even entire books to help us discover things (like themes) about the text. Biblical scholar Grant Osborne explains that a chiasm "reverses words or events in successive parallel clauses or sections."[16] In a chiasm, the text takes an ABC:CBA pattern or something similar.

Osborne illustrates this using the example of Isa 6:10 (NASB):

A. Render the hearts of this people insensitive
  B. Their ears dull
    C. and their eyes dim
    C. Lest they see with their eyes
  B. Hear with their ears
A. Understand with their hearts

Noah's flood is a giant chiasm. Gordon Wenham illustrates this structure:[17]

---

14. The Hebrew word that is transliterated as "tebah" is found in Strong's Concordance as number 8392.
15. Greidanus, *Modern Preacher and the Ancient Text*, 209.
16. Osborne, *Hermeneutical Spiral*, 39.
17. Wenham, *Word Biblical Commentary*, 148–97.

A. Noah (Gen 6:10a)
  B. Shem, Ham, and Japheth (6:10b)
    C. Ark to be built (6:14–16)
      D. Flood announced (6:17)
        E. Covenant with Noah (6:18–20)
          F. Food in the ark (6:21)
            G. Command to enter the ark (7:1–3)
              H. Seven days waiting for flood (7:4–5)
                I. Seven days waiting for flood (7:7–10)
              J. Entry to ark (7:11–15)
                K. YHWH shuts Noah in ark (7:16)
                  L. Forty days flood (7:17a)
                    M. Waters increase (7:17b–18)
                      N. Mountains covered (7:19–20)
                        O. 150 days water prevails (7:21–24)
                          P. God remembers Noah (8:1)
                        O'. 150 days water abates (8:3)
                      N' Mountain tops visible (8:4–5)
                    M'. Waters abate (8:5)
                  L'. 40 days (end of) (8:6a)
                K'. Noah opens window of ark (8:6b)
              J'. Raven and dove leave ark (8:7–9)
            I'. Seven days waiting for waters to subside (8:10–11)
          H'. Seven days waiting for waters to subside (8:12–13)
        G'. Command to leave ark (8:15–17 [22])
      F'. Food outside ark (9:1–4)
    E'. Covenant with all flesh (9:8–10)
    D'. No flood in the future (9:11–17)
  C'. Ark (9:18a)
  B'. Shem, Ham and Japheth (9:18b)
A'. Noah (9:19)

You can see the emphasis of the story of Noah from looking at the center of the chiasm. The structure builds, and at the center of the narrative you find the rather significant words: "But God remembered Noah . . . and the flood waters receded" (Gen 8:1).

Knowing how chiasm works reveals much about the text and can be discovered with a thematic outline.

APOCALYPTIC

No book on Bible interpretation is complete without at least a mention of apocalyptic literature. Unfortunately, one cannot do it justice in a short section (which is why I recommend reading the books in the footnotes to get the different perspectives). There are certain important things everyone should understand about this type of literature that I will try to summarize.

The way apocalyptic literature is interpreted is another in-house debate. Christians differ on this subject, and they all love the Lord. This is an area where we can show love for one another even when we differ. This is not to say that our lives aren't affected by how we understand this literature, but each of us should be open to exploration and dialogue about different views. Every side agrees on the big picture of the book of Revelation. Here are the major themes all the different views agree about: God's people are persecuted for their love of Him, God brings severe judgment as a result of this persecution, and Jesus comes back to rule and reign forever. Believers are to be encouraged to know that good will triumph at the end of the day, and they will find peace and rest dwelling with God forever.[18]

With this said, one must approach this literature without forgetting the rules already discussed. Interpret difficult passages encountered in light of clear passages. Look for the author's interpretation of images (e.g., the son of man is Christ in Rev 1:13, 1:18). Avoid anachronistic interpretation (reading recent news or technological developments into the symbols of Scripture). This last sentence does not rule out looking for clear signs that are not symbolic, like Jesus refers to in Matt 24 (like earthquakes and nation rising against nation). Also, take into consideration the whole

---

18. For a survey of the different major views read Jeramie Rinne's *How Will the World End? And Other Questions About the Last Things and the Second Coming of Christ*.

of Scripture when reading this literature (like seeing how Daniel, Ezekiel, and Isaiah may fit into Revelation).

The main difficulty with apocalyptic literature is how to interpret language that is so laden with symbolic imagery and figures of speech. There are a couple principles to keep in mind that can help start the process of discerning how to make sense of symbols.[19] First, symbols are of something real but refer beyond themselves. Second, find if any other passage makes clear what it is to which the symbol refers. Third, just as God can be referred to by using many symbols, so too can things in Revelation (Jesus can be the lion and a lamb). Fourth, just because part of a passage contains a symbol, it doesn't mean that the entire passage is symbolic. Lastly, it is important to discern what is and is not symbolic. Basically if something is plausible don't make it symbolic, as there is no good reason to do so. As biblical scholar Thomas Howe has written,

> In prophetic literature do not symbolize (make into a symbol) descriptions of the future that are possible or plausible (e.g., in Revelation 8:12 it is plausible that a third of the sun, moon and stars will be struck; and in Revelation 9 the locusts from the bottomless pit are a reasonable possibility as either locusts or locust-like creatures and therefore are not to be taken as symbols of the Turks), nor those descriptions that contain extensive details that would be superfluous to a symbol (e.g., the prophecy of the 144,000 in Revelation 7 contains many details about genealogies and tribal names that it becomes obvious that a symbol is not intended).[20]

---

19. These were all notes distilled from the lectures in Thomas Howe's hermeneutics class at Southern Evangelical Seminary. Inevitably, the source for these principles is reality, but it was Dr. Howe's teaching that made them clear to me.

20. Thomas Howe's unpublished class notes, "Introduction to Biblical Hermeneutics," 2002, 96.

HOW DOES GENRE HELP US UNDERSTAND?

Of course, much more can be said regarding this and every genre of literature discussed in this section.[21] It is simply beyond the scope of this book to treat these in more detail.

---

21. Fee and Stuart have a chapter on this type of literature in *How to Read the Bible for All Its Worth*. Millard J. Erickson has a great introduction called *A Basic Guide to Eschatology: Making Sense of the Millennium*. I've benefited from Robert P. Lightner's work called *The Last Days Handbook* as well. Charles Ryrie has a book called *Dispensationalism*, which deals with these issues to some extent. One great work on this subject is *An Introduction to Classical Evangelical Hermeneutics* by Mal Couch. *The Apocalypse Code* by Hank Hanegraaff is a popular presentation that foundationally disagrees with some of the other works here (but represents a well-respected position in most of the church).

6

HOW DOES LANGUAGE RELATE TO GOD?

Theologians and lay people alike have wrestled with how our language can communicate anything about God. The way one views this relationship affects how the Bible is understood. There are certain assumptions involved in the discussion that need to be exposed.

Scripture talks about God just as it claims. The difficulty we have in interpretation is that there is no unique type of language to apply to God alone. We find descriptions of God walking in the garden (Gen 3:8), parting the sea with the breath of his nostrils (Exod 15:8), and being compared to plenty of other natural things like animals, or a rock, or a fortress (Ps 18:2). It also seems like God has characteristics that are the same as those we attribute to man (feelings, etc.).

There is a tension between different verses that seem to conflict. After all, if God has these body parts then it seems like He is composed. But if God is composed, He can decompose or die. Jesus also tells us God is spirit. How do we know which is metaphor and which is literal? The assumption many have is that the metaphors are those dealing with the physical descriptions of God. However, some may say that when Jesus said God is spirit, this was a metaphor. How are these reconciled?

HOW DOES LANGUAGE RELATE TO GOD?

There are two major ways. First, one can do the hard work of making sense of an excellent defense of the classical attributes of God. Defenses like this can be found in classical sources like Thomas Aquinas or modern sources like *The Battle for God*.[1] I'd encourage everyone to push themselves to do this (perhaps in addition to Bible study). Another key way is to embrace the classical attributes and understand the different types of analogy. That is what we will explore in this chapter.

The main focus here will be explaining how analogy helps us understand God in the classical view. People use analogies when saying things like, "It is raining cats and dogs out there." Christian philosopher Max Herrera explains, "An analogy is a comparison between two things that are similar; they are the same in some respect and different in some other respect(s). For example, Jesus said that faith is like a mustard seed; they are the same in that both can be small and yet can grow into something large, but they are different in that a mustard seed is an actual kernel that grows in dirt and faith is not."[2] The reason we use analogies is because they make difficult concepts easier to grasp. These help us understand things more effectively.

Most of the statements about God that people grapple with are figures of speech, metaphors, or analogies. When the Bible describes God it uses these to help us understand Him. How you view this kind of language is largely determined by your view of God. There are two popular literary techniques in Scripture that people commonly confuse. Anthropomorphisms attribute human forms to God (e.g., walking in the garden). Anthropopathisms attribute human emotions to God (e.g., repenting, anger, etc.). Understanding these linguistic formulas, along with others, keeps us from creating God in man's image. The goal of reading certain passages where God seems to have human characteristics is to recognize what truths about the passage refer to God in his distinctive infinite way without drawing Him down to our level.[3] Understanding analogy also helps

---

1. Geisler, House, and Herrera, *Battle For God*.
2. Herrera, "Using Analogies to Reach the Lost and Refute the Cults," 10.
3. Clarke, *The One and the Many*, 54.

us avoid the extremes of agnosticism, which says we can know nothing of God and making God just a bigger version of us.

It is commonly acknowledged that to understand God we must grasp some concepts about Him. Just as in the analogy between the mustard seed and faith, there is something the same and an aspect that is different in our ideas of how God is. The way to discover what is identical and what differs depends on the nature of reality. Part of our analysis is to look at how different things exist (both God and creation). When doing so, one can discover there are four ways to use language to apply to God. Understanding these helps us to discern which the Bible may be using in order to understand God.[4]

ANALOGY OF CAUSE AND EFFECT

The first we will examine is the analogy where the effect is like the cause.[5] In this type of analogy there are two things compared—the effect and cause.[6] When I heat water and it has an egg in it, the egg gets hot because the water is hot. This would be a case where the effect is like the cause.

Scriptures expresses that we can know certain things about God because of things we see in creation. Rom 1:20 says, "For since the creation of the world God's invisible qualities—his eternal power and divine nature—have been clearly seen, being understood from what has been made, so that people are without excuse." Here we are told that what is invisible is seen. In Ps 19:1 it is written, "The heavens declare the glory of God; the skies proclaim the work of his hands." Much about God is known from what He has created. These verses tell us that creation speaks of God's existence and attributes.

---

4. For more formal treatments, see analogy in Henry Koren's *An Introduction to the Science of Metaphysics*, Norman Geisler's *Systematic Theology*, and Battista Mondin's *The Principle of Analogy in Protestant and Catholic Theology*.

5. This is called the analogy of intrinsic attribution.

6. For each of these types of analogies, the things compared in the literature are called analogates.

The reason we can ascertain these things is because there is something similar between creation and the Creator. Because creation is intelligible, one can discover that God is also intelligible. Insofar as creation is beautiful, it communicates that God is beautiful. When people ascertain other attributes of God from His creation their language implies this type of analogy.

This way of understanding also explains the immanence of God (i.e., God is present to all His effects). People see aspects of the divine from looking at created things. One must be careful not to confuse the two, but to learn what you can from what God reveals of Himself through creation. Those who use only this type of analogy are pantheists (who believe all is God). They have failed to recognize the real difference between God and what He has made.

ANALOGY OF DIFFERENCE

In this type of analogy, the effect is completely different from the cause.[7] Only cause and effect are compared. Atheists note the evil in the world. They say this proves if God is like creation, He must be evil. This type of analogy explains very clearly how the atheist is wrong.

One of the most famous cases of failing to understand this is found in the agnostic philosopher David Hume. He asks the believer to consider all the imperfections in the world. If you really want to make the case that an effect resembles the cause, God may be likened to a "stupid mechanic" who really doesn't know how to create things.[8]

Hume failed to understand that there are different types of analogy. There are certain things about the world that are dissimilar from God. The Christian responds that the evil and imperfections we see is not like the cause of the world. Consider other cases where an effect is not like its cause.

---

7. This is called the analogy of extrinsic attribution.
8. Hume, *The Empiricists*, 464–65.

Look at an egg and water. When an egg is heated in the water the egg gets hard. But the water is not hard. This is a clear case where the effect is not like its cause.

Also, look at an artist and her picture. Think of the artist that paints a picture of a field. The artist is not like the material aspects (i.e., paint, canvas) of the picture, and one can imagine many ways she is not like the painted field.

Thus, if one considers a flower, which has petals and roots, it is in no way necessary to say God also has those. Similar to the others mentioned, these are examples where the effect is not like its cause. In the literature this is called the analogy of extrinsic attribution.

This type of analogy explains how the creation is unlike God. Using this analogy, theologians explain the transcendence of God from creation. Those who use only this type of analogy are deists (who say God is completely other—creation is completely unlike its Creator). If a person refuses to recognize any other type of analogy but this one, then they end up in agnosticism (as nothing in creation tells us anything about God) or mysticism (as God can only directly reveal himself to you through a mystical experience). All of these options (deism, agnosticism, and mysticism) undermine the nature and sufficiency of the Bible as a revelation of God.

ANALOGY OF ACTION

This type compares four things.[9] The action is what is primarily emphasized and compared in this type of analogy. This is commonly known as metaphor. Many standardized tests use this type of analogy to see how people relate concepts. They say something like, "Armies are to nations as the Bible is to Christians." Both are needed for the survival of the two groups being compared. Focus on the *action* of relating how A is to B, and C is to D. In Scripture, the parable of the unjust judge is an example where this type of analogy is present. In Luke 18:1–8 (NIV) we read,

---

9. This is called the analogy of improper proportionality.

HOW DOES LANGUAGE RELATE TO GOD?

> Then Jesus told his disciples a parable to show them that they should always pray and not give up. He said: "In a certain town there was a judge who neither feared God nor cared what people thought. And there was a widow in that town who kept coming to him with the plea, 'Grant me justice against my adversary.' "For some time he refused. But finally he said to himself, 'Even though I don't fear God or care what people think, yet because this widow keeps bothering me, I will see that she gets justice, so that she won't eventually come and attack me!'" And the Lord said, "Listen to what the unjust judge says. And will not God bring about justice for his chosen ones, who cry out to him day and night? Will he keep putting them off? I tell you, he will see that they get justice, and quickly. However, when the Son of Man comes, will he find faith on the earth?"

The widow in this parable is being compared to the person praying. Who is the unjust judge being compared to? We can readily see he is compared to God. It is not that Jesus's comparison means he is emphasizing that God is unjust, but that God's *action* will be like that of the unjust judge who grants justice to the widow. The point is that God will grant justice to those praying without ceasing (in verse 1 above). The argument here is that if an unjust judge grants justice because of ceaseless petition, how much more will the just judge of the universe grant justice?

Consider this Scripture: "As the deer pants for the water so my soul longs after thee." There are four things compared here. The deer is like my soul. The deer's desire and longing for water is like our longing and desire for God. The deer is yearning for that which can fulfill in the same way that our soul yearns for that which can fulfill. Again, it is the action that is emphasized in this type of analogy.

This type of analogy is evident in Scriptures where God is called a rock, a door, a lion, or even where God shelters you under his wings. We don't think God is made of stone, but that He is unmoving. We don't think that God has a handle, but that He opens our way. We don't think He is a giant feline, but is strong and ferocious in battle. God is not a giant hen, but is a comfort to those whose walk is blameless. Each of these metaphors should be understood properly so that we can know God.

ANALOGY OF PROPER NATURES

This analogy also compares four things.[10] As the nature of A is to B, so also the nature of C is to D. Infinite goodness is to infinite being as finite goodness is to finite being. The infinite is not compared to the finite here. The infinite is only compared to the infinite and the finite to the finite. We are only looking at the nature of the thing. The good tree is to providing oxygen, shade, and beauty as the good wife is to Prov 31.

There are certain attributes of God that primarily belong to Him and only secondarily apply to created things. These would include being, activity, power, unity, wisdom, goodness, and love. W. Norris Clarke explains that each attribute signifies activities similar in God and creatures, without explaining how each performs them.[11] This explanation accounts for how certain attributes can apply to both us and God given our differences with God.

There are various terms like goodness, being, unity, power, etc., which are called transcendentals. They go above (i.e., transcend) each of the categories of existing things and apply to each of them according to how they exist. In this explanation of analogy we can say that the way a term is applied is in accordance with its nature. We don't denigrate a person by attributing the same descriptive term to them and to something that has significantly less value. Everyone recognizes that a wife is of greater value than a tree, and we shouldn't be hesitant to apply the term "good" to both when appropriate. This analogy explains why it is reasonable to do so.

---

10. This is called the analogy of proper proportionality.
11. Clarke, *The One and the Many*, 54–55.

HOW DOES LANGUAGE RELATE TO GOD?

TYPES OF ANALOGY AND KNOWING GOD

This chapter explained how we know God. God has revealed Himself in creation and in Scripture. The four types of analogy help us to discern how language relates to God. Understanding these figures of speech are among the most difficult things you'll encounter in interpretation. The work to do this can also be among the most rewarding undertaking while exploring how to know God.

The richness in understanding divine attributes from studying His creation is due to the types of analogy. W. Norris Clarke clarifies that each creation has a similarity to each other and to God who is their source. He writes,

> This similarity in difference is the participation structure of all finite beings as participating intrinsically, in various finite ways, in the infinite fullness of perfection of God himself as the Creative Source of all being.... In a word, the analogous term (thought and word) gives linguistic expression to an objective metaphysical structure of participation: many real beings possessing in various limited ways a common attribute, received from a common source, which possesses the same attribute in unlimited fullness.[12]

Our thoughts and words hold together similarity and dissimilarity between creation and the Creator. God is infinite and boundless perfection in unlimited existence. In creation we find instances of limited and finite creatures having various degrees of perfection within them. The full perfection of any attribute can only be in God. In creation you'll find the perfection of each attribute only applied analogically. Analogy explains how to relate qualities found in creation to God.

Needless to say, we use analogies every day. The aforementioned types of analogy can help us as we examine passages that seem daunting to decipher. In order to have a quick reference for what I've tried to briefly state, here is a chart of the four types:

---

12. Ibid., 56.

TYPE OF ANALOGY	NUMBER OF THINGS COMPARED	MAIN EMPHASIS COMPARED	EXAMPLES
Cause and Effect	Two	Effect and cause similar	The egg and water are hot
Difference	Two	Effect and cause differ	The egg is hard, but not the water
Action	Four	Action	A rock imperfectly resembles the action of God
Nature	Four	Nature of things compared	A creature is good (qualified) and God is unrestricted goodness

7

AVOIDING LAND MINES IN INTERPRETATION

If you ever have to walk through a minefield, you'll want to have a map revealing where there are dangers. Similarly, there are common places we should avoid that are hazard areas for interpretation. Everyone can recognize the variety of resources at our disposal that aid our understanding of Scripture. Even given the resources in this book, there are typical errors one can find in many books on hermeneutics and the Bible. The best way to avoid falling prey to these common errors is to know them up front. Remember while becoming familiar with these that knowledge does not equal spiritual maturity. As mentioned, these mistakes are so typical it is likely that even our favorite Bible teachers may have fallen into confusion on one of these points at some time. Therefore, in order to inoculate us from misunderstanding the Scripture, focus for a few pages on the most common fallacious approaches to interpreting the Bible.

PSYCHOANALYSIS FALLACY

This is the fallacy that one has to get into the mind of the author in order to understand the text. Somehow, one is to read the author's mind. You'll hear this expressed as the sentiment, "You have to understand the author's intention in order to ascertain the meaning of the text." However, if the author's intention is in his mind (which it is undoubtedly), and the author isn't here (which none of the biblical authors are), then there is no way to truly ever know the meaning. Due to the unfortunate error of this reasoning, one can never know anything that a person says (even if they are with us) as we can never be in their mind (which is required to know the intention).

The problem is that it is impossible to ever get into the author's mind independent of what he has told us. An individual tells us the intentions of her mind through spoken or written words. There is no other way to communicate.

It may be the case that when someone says we need to know the author's intention, what we should look for is *why* something is written. The meaning of what is written can be known independently of knowing why it is written. You can know what I say even if you don't know why I say it. I may tell you, "Leave the building quickly!" You can know the objective meaning of my command even if you have no clue as to the reason why. If I choose to tell you why I said something, it can provide further explanation. However, it is *not* necessary to understand the meaning of the text of Scripture to know why certain things are said. To say I must know why a person said something in order to know what they are saying is to commit the psychoanalysis fallacy.

WORD STUDY FALLACIES

There are many types of "word study fallacies." For a fantastic introduction to these, consider picking up D. A. Carson's *Exegetical Fallacies*, where he explains sixteen of them. Something common is that all of them 1) investigate the range of meaning of a word, and 2) give the word the wrong meaning. People do so when giving a meaning that is foreign to the actual context of the way a word is used in the sentence.

If one ignores that there are many possible meanings for many words, and also ignores the grammar, then the circumstances are favorable for committing this fallacy. Remember that context determines the meaning. The context includes the syntax—which is the grammar.

In addition, if a person knows only a little Greek or Hebrew, due to the amazing resources that make much of the original meaning accessible, there is a pull people feel to show off (amazingly even by pastors!). D. A. Carson sheds light on the main reason these fallacies are so prevalent.

> Perhaps the principle reason why word studies constitute a particularly rich source for exegetical fallacies is that many preachers and Bible teachers know Greek only well enough to use concordances, or perhaps a little more. There is little feel for what has been learned in study, which as often as not is a great deal of lexical information without the restraining influence of context.[1]

Thus, the danger is present when one arbitrarily picks among several meanings while ignoring the context where the word is used.

One of the most common word study fallacies is the root fallacy. It basically looks at the root or etymology of a given word as determinative of its meaning. The etymology of a word is the original meaning that the word had. Those that commit this fallacy often break a word into different parts and say the "real" meaning is simply putting those parts together. Assuming the loss of some English words, a person using this method one thousand years in the future would think we park on the parkway and drive on the driveway. This is the root fallacy.

ERROR OF ALLEGORIZING

The allegorical method has been around since at least the time of Origen (3rd century AD). This method seeks to go beneath the meaning of the text for a deeper or "real" meaning. The true meaning, in this account, is not found in what is plainly on the surface of what is communicated. Instead, this says there is a meaning

---

1. Carson, *Exegetical Fallacies*, 64.

beyond what is normally understood that needs to be grasped. Those using this approach, for example, would say the Song of Solomon is really about Christ and the church.

There are significant problems with this approach. First, by failing to account for the historical context it distorts the meaning of the text. In distorting the text it changes the message God is delivering to people. A second problem is that a person explaining a deeper meaning underlying the text (that is different from what is plainly communicated) expects you to *not* look for a deeper meaning in their own text (that is different from what they are communicating).

ERROR OF SPIRITUALIZING

This error takes place when discarding the earthly, physical, historical reality and crosses to a spiritual analogy. Like when one allegorizes everything, this takes away from what the text is actually communicating. For example, Jesus stilling the storm becomes spiritualized to "storms on the sea of life." The "spiritual" transfer only takes one or two elements of the text and ignores other parts of the text that may be really important to grasp the meaning. Consider a parallel. You ask a chemist what something is, and he explains the properties of the two elements he has discovered are hydrogen and oxygen. He says nothing more of what it is, and you surmise that this must be H_2O (water), so you drink it. However, suppose the chemist leaves some of the elements out. The substance could also be sulfuric acid (H_2SO_4). The one won't harm you, and the other will kill you. Leaving out significant elements of the Scripture changes the meaning.

In committing this error the text also becomes subjective and arbitrary. Those using the approach can make the text mean practically anything as the text no longer limits the meaning. Scripture ceases to be a reliable guide for faith and daily living when this approach is adopted.

AVOIDING LAND MINES IN INTERPRETATION

ERROR OF MORALIZING

This error consists of drawing moral inferences (usually things to do or become) from every text of Scripture. With the Scripture under consideration, moralizing asks, "what's the moral of this story?" It then focuses on the character or his actions to make a moral point. The problem here is by focusing on these elements one may miss the real point of the story. It may be true that a person did something or was a certain way, but most of the time this is not relevant. To make it so is to not grasp what God is communicating in the story.

Some will point out that there are virtues, vices, and moral lessons taught in Scripture. Of course this is true. The ethical demands may also reveal something about God. However, moralizing emphasizes what is of secondary importance and ignores the context of God's word. So, if the virtues of an individual are not grounded in the context of what God is communicating, it takes away from the message we should receive.

Perhaps the worst mistake with this error is it confuses the descriptive passages of Scripture with the prescriptive. A descriptive passage tells you what happened. A prescriptive passage tells you something about how you ought to act. This mistake can be devastating to many. Take the following hypothetical scenario. A college football team never shows up to the championship game. When reporters went to explore what happened to the team, they found the entire team got confused between the prescriptive and descriptive signs on the highway. The team not only got off at every exit, they cleaned every restroom between their home and the football field. Here is an example of moralizing offered by Sidney Greidanus:

MORALIZING	OUR RESPONSE
Jesus asks, "Do you love me?"	Do we love him
Peter says, "Yes, Lord"	Our response should be
Jesus commands, "Feed my sheep."	We have a task[C]

  C. Greidanus, *Modern Preacher and the Ancient Text*, 164.

ERROR OF FOCUSING ON "THE FACTS"

This happens when one spends time on proving that the events or details in the Bible did or did not take place. We should never allow apologetics to replace Bible study. Remember, it is what we learn from the word of God that saves us. Another problem with this is that it ignores what the text is actually saying and emphasizes only the historical aspects. These historical aspects can be important for understanding the meaning of the text, but should never replace the focus of our study, which is to uncover what the text means.

ERROR OF IMITATING BIBLE CHARACTERS

This approach asks us to imitate certain people and study detailed aspects of their life. It asks us to bridge the gap between the characters of history and us today. Recognize that *most* of the Bible never asks us to imitate another human. One of the major problems this approach makes is it transforms biblical description (of what certain people did) into prescription (how we ought to be). One has to be careful to take the universal elements away from narratives where biblical characters are found and *not* to focus on imitating the specifics. For example, we find Abraham is a person who walks by faith. This is what we are told to imitate—walking by faith and not by sight. We are not to imitate other aspects of his life (e.g., having children with a woman who is not your wife, etc.).

This approach is criticized as an anthropocentric (meaning human-centered) interpretation. This simply means that the interpretation focuses on human characters—their characteristics or good and evil deeds. This may lead one to have the tendency of shifting the attention to man and away from God. Remember that the Bible is given to reveal to us things about God. Unfortunately, when the focus is primarily on humans in the text it draws attention away from God. It also makes the Bible on par with any other book recording human acts.

AVOIDING LAND MINES IN INTERPRETATION

CONFUSING THE ROLE OF THE HOLY SPIRIT

Many books on biblical interpretation mention that the Holy Spirit is necessary for Bible study. Insofar as we can cannot live, move, or breathe aside from God sustaining us this is true. God took Nebuchadnezzar's ability to reason because of his pride (Dan 4:30–36). So, due to mankind's complete dependence upon God for our continued existence, we do need God to sustain us while studying Scripture.

Nevertheless, we must recognize that it is not the Holy Spirit's responsibility that humans understand Scripture. People have to study and learn to grasp God's word better. This is the reason to learn how to interpret the Bible. There are many elements in this book—all of which the Holy Spirit knows—that need to be learned to be more effective in seeing what God is communicating. For example, knowledge of grammar and figures of speech are needed to help a person understand the meaning of Scripture. Many of those who teach spend countless hours of their life devoted to learning the original languages of the Bible. The Holy Spirit knows Hebrew, Greek, and every language. Mankind does not without study.

We can draw a distinction that may help us to understand the role of the Holy Spirit. The Holy Spirit does not tell us what the text says. If He did, there would be no need to study to understand Scripture (but there is a need to study!). The Holy Spirit applies what you've understood from the text to convict you of sin, and righteousness, and judgment (John 16:8–11).

When godly Bible teachers disagree about interpretation, both having the Holy Spirit indwelling them, one has to look for the reasons *why* each person holds their interpretation is better than those that differ. The message of the Bible, *what* it says, is the meaning that anyone who is not mentally incapacitated (even if they do not have the Holy Spirit!) can understand. This comports well with the fact that many non-Christians can understand the Scriptures—even though they reject it.

Recognize that the fact the Holy Spirit does not interpret for us should not keep us from praying for wisdom and help from

God. Certainly God allows us to put certain things together that we may have been struggling with for long periods of time. He can bring to mind things that were forgotten or have us come across resources that help us in our studies. God may even motivate you to pick up resources listed in the bibliography in order to understand His word better. Our prayers for God's help are answered more frequently than we realize. I'll leave you with a final prayer that many believers have had God answer. This is the "Prayer Before Study" by Thomas Aquinas.

> Ineffable Creator, Who, from the treasures of Your wisdom has established three hierarchies of angels, has arrayed them in marvelous order above the fiery heavens, and has marshaled the regions of the universe with such artful skill, You are proclaimed the true font of light and wisdom, and the primal origin raised high beyond all things. Pour forth a ray of Your brightness into the darkened places of my mind; disperse from my soul the twofold darkness into which I was born: sin and ignorance. You make eloquent the tongues of infants. Refine my speech and pour forth upon my lips the goodness of Your blessing. Grant to me keenness of mind, capacity to remember, skill in learning, subtlety to interpret, and eloquence in speech. May You guide the beginning of my work, direct its progress, and bring it to completion. You Who are true God and true Man, Who live and reign, world without end. Amen.

8

LOVE STORY FROM THE BATTLEFIELD

BIBLICAL APPLICATION

WE KNOW THAT IDEAS have consequences. To this point in the book we've been examining how to glean the ideas that God is communicating through His word. What you believe about God and what He has revealed affects how you will act. There are overarching principles in Scripture that establish how to view the world. The principles and ideas of the Bible, which are grounded in reality, are given to help guide our thoughts and actions.

Some describe the Bible as unpacking a wonderful love story complete with all the characters. The characters, though many, include a damsel in distress, a villain, and a hero. The biblical narrative can be understood as a greater story of which we all play a part. It is not difficult to find language in Scripture of God's bride (Israel) who is under attack—with the hope that God will rescue her when all seems lost. A war is waging around us. The primary villain is Satan, but he has many servants that join his crusade to destroy. God does more than give His servants instruction that allows them to merely survive the assault. He equips them with every good thing they need to flourish, along with strategies of how to recruit others to join. Putting to work the faith with which you were entrusted is the subject of application.

The greatest difficulty in application is combining it with motivation. Many people leave church each week satisfied that they heard a good sermon, but still feel something is missing. After Abraham Lincoln once lamented a pastor's sermon was not great, he was asked why he thought that way. He noted that the pastor failed to call people to action. It is also reported in ancient times that "when Cicero had finished speaking, the people said, 'How well he spoke,' but when Demosthenes had finished speaking, they said, 'Let us march.'"[1] A major goal of this chapter is to provide your marching orders that include both application and motivation.

There is no doubt the subject of application is multifaceted. After ensuring that the meaning of the text is known, the next stage is to begin to apply what is said to particular circumstances. Think of this as receiving instructions of what to do upon coming to the realization that you are in the middle of a battlefield. Realize also that the application will be only as good as the foundation for it in the actual meaning of the text. If you have missed the meaning of a particular Scripture, then you're unlikely to properly act. Nevertheless, universal principles in the Bible apply even if you may have improperly grasped one particular passage.

It is important to recognize two levels of the application question: the universal and the particular. The universal action deals with the general principles gleaned from a passage. The particular action you take in certain circumstances is where you'd find the need to employ these principles. For example, love your neighbor is a general or universal principle. The particular ways this is worked out refer to the many ways to love my neighbor (like bringing them soup when they are sick, shoveling their drive if it has snowed, or writing them a word of encouragement).

We will briefly glance at other issues in application every person will face. The following things are vital to keep in mind to

---

1. Martin, *Adlai Stevenson and the World*, 549.

guide your journey. They will hopefully provide some inspiration to stand against the forces of darkness that seek our destruction.

SCRIPTURE AS A GUIDE

In living for Christ, the Scripture is to be our preeminent guide for life.[2] Paul states it clearly and succinctly: "All Scripture is God-breathed and is useful for teaching, rebuking, correcting, and training in righteousness, so that the man of God may be thoroughly equipped for every good work" (2 Tim 3:16–17). From this reference many people have surmised that the Bible guides believers in every area necessary to live a godly life. If the Christian wants to be thoroughly equipped for every good work, he ought to know the whole counsel of God revealed in His word.

The view that God's word is sufficient for all that believers need for faith and practice is undermined at the popular level with three words: "God told me." People that say "God told them," either mean 1) that God has revealed in His word what to do, 2) that God spoke to them in an audible voice, or 3) that they think God is telling them something through the emotions or feelings they have when thinking about something. The third option may also include certain "fleeces" (based on what Gideon does in Judges), where a person tests God by asking for signs. For example, if God wants me to go to church, let me catch all green lights on the way. On the other hand, if God wants me to go to breakfast with friends, then let me catch a red light. I've even heard some Christians use the example of asking God whether to stay with or break up with a person depending on how long it takes them to answer a phone!

We can exclude analysis of the first (which supports using Scripture as guidance) and focus on problems with number two. The second is that God spoke in an audible voice. Two questions are apparent: 1) How do you know it was God, and 2) how does what you heard compare with what Scripture reveals? The Bible

---

2. Many principles in this chapter are gleaned from Garry Friesen's book *Decision Making and the Will of God*. I highly recommend both this book and Greg Koukl's discussion on the same topic.

reveals that there are different entities—not all benevolent—that can speak to you in an audible voice. Some of these may be deceiving. After all, Satan masquerades as an angel of light (2 Cor 11:14). Christians are told to test the spirits to make sure they are from God (1 John 4:1). Certainly this test spoken of can only come from comparing what guidance is given with what the Scripture says. If it doesn't conflict (meaning it is not immoral or heretical), then you still can legitimately question whether it is God or Satan that is speaking. God confirms His message in Scripture with true miracles (Moses in Egypt, Elijah on Mt. Carmel). Certainly it is not unreasonable for Him to confirm an audible voice with a true miracle. These are opposed to counterfeit signs and wonders that some will be deceived by in the end times (Matt 24:24). In Heb 1:1–2 we find there is no longer a need for prophets: "In the past God spoke to our ancestors through the prophets at many times and in various ways, but in these last days he *has spoken* to us by his Son, whom he appointed heir of all things, and through whom also he made the universe." Note by my emphasis that "has spoken" in verse 2 is past tense.

Let's explore some issues with number three (that God is speaking through your feelings or through "fleeces"). First, the Scripture is clear that the heart of man is deceitful and as such is easy to manipulate (Jer 17:9). It is much easier to observe people attributing their subjective feelings to being a message of God. Upon encountering people clearly violating what their emotions or "fleeces" said God told them to do, I've asked why they are not still doing what God told them to do several weeks before. The common response is that now God is telling them something completely opposite of what He originally told them. The main problem with this language is it elevates subjective feelings and thoughts to the level of the word of God. In this model, God also ends up looking fickle, unwise, and unable to tell what is going on from one moment to the next.

There are other problems with using "fleeces" to discern God's will about what we should do. Gideon *knew* what God's will was already. He used the fleece simply to verify *that God would be with him.* Also, Gideon was trying to get out of the responsibility that God had placed upon him. He was afraid to do what God commanded. The verification with the fleece wasn't to tell whether God wanted him to go or not. It was simply that God would save Israel by Gideon's hand. Here is the text from Judg 6:36–37:

> Gideon said to God, "If you will save Israel by my hand as you have promised—look, I will place a wool fleece on the threshing floor. If there is dew only on the fleece and all the ground is dry, then I will know that you will save Israel by my hand, as you said. (NIV)

Another significant problem is that Gideon's fleeces each validated God's message because what happened was a genuine miracle. Remember what happens in Judg 6. God told Gideon He would save Israel by Gideon's hand. Gideon says to God, I'll believe you'll do this if you make the wool fleece completely wet and the ground all around it is dry. He got a bowl of water from the fleece and the ground was dry. Then Gideon made another request; make the ground wet and the fleece completely dry (which God did). These requests asked God to confirm His message through the miracles of the fleece.

If we want to extract a real parallel to Gideon's fleece, then ask for genuine miracles to confirm extra-biblical messages from God. You may say this to the Lord when using your own miraculous fleece for discernment: "If you want me to X (anything can go in place of X—marrying a person, going to a particular school, taking a job, etc.), then spin around my computer clockwise in the air." You'll also have to give a negative, "If you *don't* want me to X, make my computer spin around counterclockwise in the air." Now if neither of these happen, then God isn't necessarily talking to you or even thinking you should be using these "fleeces" to help you make decisions. In using everyday things as "fleeces" (let me see a cardinal today, God, if you want me to move to the state that has the cardinal as the state bird), you've abused the point of this story and have failed to see the real truth you can take away. First, Gideon's asking for a sign was a mark of his unbelief. This is hardly a good example to follow. Second, if you did want to follow his example, then by *not* asking for a truly miraculous sign you've missed the most crucial part of how Gideon knows it is really God answering.

There are ways to get guidance that don't require asking for miraculous signs. I counsel those desiring instruction to have a familiarity with what the Bible actually says regarding the issues with which they struggle. There are many areas where God's word gives very clear guidance. We can use a concordance or even search quickly online to see what the Bible says about many moral areas. For example, if you want to know whether to engage in occult activity, you'll find clear condemnation in Scripture against this. The problem we most often have is that we rely on subjective feelings to tell us what to do, say God is telling us, and elevate our personal preferences to the level of what God has revealed.

The Bible gives a general process believers can use to seek guidance. First, God instructs everyone regarding what they ought to do morally (call this God's moral will). Second, God also expects you to seek wisdom from others (the point of the wisdom literature). Third, one may pray to ask for aid in helping us discern certain facets of what is involved in the decision. Fourth, take into consideration your personal preferences as to what is involved.

Let's explore the first way to consider the moral boundaries explained in the word of God. Think of them as drawing limits around areas that we are not allowed to cross. It may be helpful to picture them as a guardrail that protects you from plummeting to your death or destruction. Scripture also gives guidance about what to do when it doesn't make crystal clear the morality of a certain behavior.

In cases that seem to be less clear about what to do, the Proverbs say you should seek guidance from the wise. You can use wisdom gathered from many godly sources to try to find the best answer. The pooled insight of many can give more alternatives and a fresh perspective.

As mentioned, personal preferences are important, especially when the area is not a moral issue. For example, the Scripture is clear with its guidance about who a believer can marry. If you choose to marry, it must be a fellow believer of the opposite sex.

The role wisdom plays in selecting a spouse is that you should make sure to marry one who has discretion: "Like a gold ring in a pig's snout is a beautiful woman without discretion" (Prov 11:22). You not only get the gold ring, you get a pig too. This is something you should try to avoid. There can be many options of quality mates that meet this standard. This is where you have freedom based on your tastes. There is also another thing to realize with this guideline. It is not a sin to marry someone who lacks discretion, but it is *foolish* to do so.

LOVE IS ALWAYS RIGHT

Jesus has explained that the two greatest commandments are to love God and to love others. Our love for God is to be with the entirety of our being—heart, soul, mind, and strength (Luke 10:27). It is our love for the Lord that is to be primary, as He is the perfect one completely worthy of the whole of our being. Our souls will never find rest until it rests in Him. It is because of God that we live and move and have our being. He is the source and sustainer of all that exists, the Creator and Holy one, the God of Abraham, Isaac, and Jacob. His love for us is everlasting, and His mercies are new every morning. As holy, God cannot tolerate sin, but the Lord gave His son to restore us to a relationship with Himself. As believers we can again have a relationship with our Creator and live as we ought. God has given us divine power. Peter explains:

> His divine power has given us everything we need for a godly life through our knowledge of him who called us by his own glory and goodness. Through these he has given us his very great and precious promises, so that through them you may participate in the divine nature, having escaped the corruption in the world caused by evil desires. For this very reason, make every effort to add to your faith goodness; and to goodness, knowledge; and to knowledge, self-control; and to self-control, perseverance; and to perseverance, godliness; and to godliness, mutual affection; and to mutual affection, love. For if you possess these qualities in increasing measure, they will keep you

from being ineffective and unproductive in your knowledge of our Lord Jesus Christ. But whoever does not have them is nearsighted and blind, forgetting that they have been cleansed from their past sins. (2 Pet 1:3–9)

Although the mantra of the day has many believing self-esteem is our major barrier to effectiveness, it is really the lack of our love for others. Consider two popular admonitions: Love your neighbor as yourself; do unto others as you would have done to you. Both of these not only presuppose that you love yourself, but also that your actions to others are based on the way you love yourself! The way to start exercising this love for others is to focus differently than what most of the world has advised. Whereas the world tells people to look inwardly and at the past to help us become effective, the Bible guides us to look outwardly and upwardly. This is an important contrast to recognize. It is clear that some people spend time on a counselor's couch examining their own hearts along with talking about and reliving their past. This may be somewhat beneficial. However, we must not stop there. The Christian life is to be lived, there are hearts to be won, and there are battles to be fought. Focusing upwardly helps us to see the nature of God and the fact He is the one to whom the battle belongs. Focusing outwardly helps us not meditate on our own selfish and sinful hearts and instead gets us loving and serving others. Many have experienced the freedom that comes from loving others and taking up the cross of self-sacrifice. These believers have discovered the truth in the radical paradox that whoever finds his life will lose it, and whoever loses his life for my sake will find it (Matt 10:39).

DECISION-MAKING WHEN CHRISTIANS DIFFER

How should we act when Christians differ about a subject? Some of the things available today were not around thousands of years ago, so we may be uncertain how to approach certain topics. For example, there were no pianos, radios, televisions, or movies when the authors of Scripture wrote. On the other hand, there are things Christians disagree about that *are* written in Scripture, and we need wisdom about how to handle these as well (like drinking alcohol, for example). What does the Scripture say?

The fourteenth chapter of Romans is where we can all turn for guidance in these issues. Paul is writing to believers about this very subject—decision making when Christians differ. His guidance is basically that we should love others and do whatever we can to keep them from sinning. When something is not clearly forbidden, each person should be fully convinced in his own mind what is right to do because we will give an account of ourselves to God (Rom 14:5, 12). We are always to act in love and in ways that bring peace and mutual edification (15–19). Those that are stronger (realizing what is and is not sin) should avoid doing anything that causes a brother to stumble into sin (14:20—15:2). This is the general way to approach issues about which Christians disagree. Christ gave us the example we are to follow through His self-sacrifice.

A WORD OF WARNING ABOUT BIBLE READING

It may seem odd to include a warning about studying the Bible in a chapter about application of the Scripture. However, there are real dangers associated with the knowledge you've acquired from this book. There are not only dangers associated with incorrect interpretation and application, but also associated with correct interpretation. I think that being aware of these dangers is a good start in helping us to avoid them. After all, we've been told that "the truth will set you free" (John 8:32).

First, let's look at some of the dangers of incorrect interpretation. In general, one can sum up all these dangers in the phrase, "Ideas have consequences." Improper understanding of God's word can not only be spiritually dangerous, but it can also be physically dangerous.

One obvious danger is that heresy may arise when people improperly interpret the Bible. It is certainly possible to be a Christian and have the wrong interpretation of parts of Scripture. However, when groups hold views that reject an essential Christian doctrine, cults are formed. For example, Jehovah's Witnesses hold that Deut 6:4—"Hear, O Israel: The Lord our God, the Lord is one"—rules out the doctrine of the Trinity. However, the oneness of the Godhead in this verse establishes one of the central tenets of the Trinity. So, far from this disproving the Trinity, this reference, known to the Hebrews as the *Shema*, affirms an element essential to understanding the Trinity (namely, the oneness of God).

One may also recognize that some people will reject the Bible altogether due to a poor approach to interpretation. The reason for this is not everyone who reads the Bible has the tools necessary to properly understand it (something that by this point in the book should be no problem for you). For example, some struggle with seeming contradictions and difficult passages they find in the biblical texts. So, for example, one Gospel says that shepherds came to visit Jesus at a stable (Luke 2:16), and another says that wise men came to visit him at a house (Matt 2:11). Another text states we are saved "by grace, through faith, not by works" (Eph 2:8), and yet another says we are "to work out our salvation with fear and trembling" (Phil 2:12). Contrary to the critics, there are ways to reconcile and understand these verses that show their harmony.

One of the most concerning risks of improperly understanding the text is that those who teach truths about God are judged more severely (Jas 3:1; Matt 12:36). Not only is there a stricter judgment for teachers, but God may punish those who misrepresent Him (Job 42:8). This could possibly be one of the greatest motivations to ensure that we properly apply the methods outlined in this work to understand God's word.

Another hazard of wrong interpretation is that it leads to dangerous behavior. For example, some take Isa 53:5, "by his wounds we are healed," to be an admonition to avoid medicine and medical care once you've trusted Jesus. With the rise and spread of many types of physical ailments, it should be obvious why these types of behaviors should be a great concern for the welfare of those who have the wrong belief about what the Scripture teaches here.

Every person who teaches others how to interpret their Bible should also consider the dangers associated with the correct interpretation. This is the aspect that is often overlooked. There are a couple of things that may be noted in relation to this warning.

First, people tend to confuse understanding the text with being spiritually mature. Those that fall into this think that since they've understood what is said it is equivalent to having applied that knowledge to life. Moreover, it is but a small step to think you are better than others because you've understood something another has not. Many, without realizing it, slip into this way of thinking and develop a sinful pride that the Scripture says to guard against. The Bible teaches individuals are to value others over themselves (Rom 12:3; Phil 2:3). Also consider the warning that "knowledge puffs up, but love builds up" (1 Cor 8:1). This is *not* to say that these are mutually exclusive. Simply recognize the warning against being puffed up with pride because we know something another person does not. We must not confuse spiritual maturity with understanding. Pride is a vice we must guard against.

A second problem may be that the person who thinks he properly understands the text may be closed to the possibility of correction. As sinful and fallen creatures, we have a propensity for evil and error. However, once we've started understanding some things that others have missed, it is possible to be more apt to dismiss what others say when they admonish us from the Scripture. We need a true assessment of ourselves.

THE MOTIVATION FOR CHRISTIAN LIVING

God has placed in each man a vacuum that only He can fill. However, there are other desires men have during this life that drive their actions each day. Some value money, pleasure, and honor. In themselves these things are not bad, but none of them can fully satisfy. Money is simply a means to an end (the *love* of money is the root of all kinds of evil as it supplants love for people and for God). We are to love people and use things, not vice versa. We must recognize that we long for truth, goodness, and beauty. Our longing for these three things are insatiable during this life. It is only when we see the one God that is infinite truth, goodness, and beauty that we will rest.

However, God realizes that people have other desires that help motivate them to action. After all, we are not only called to salvation, but to share in the rewards Jesus will give upon his return.[3] Once you become a Christ-follower, you should be like a faithful and wise servant, a wise virgin prepared to meet the bridegroom, and a wise servant that faithfully invests the talents he has been given (Matt 24–25). In doing so, you earn rewards and share in your master's happiness when he returns. If you don't do so, you'll not receive a reward and will suffer loss. You will be saved, but only as one that escapes through the flames (1 Cor 3:10–15). We should not overlook this important motivating factor for loving and serving others (especially since God uses it in the Scripture to motivate).

There is also a fear factor for those who don't do good works. It is true that perfect love drives out fear. But believers who do not abide in Christ will not experience this perfect love in this life. Many fear death, and others fear judgment. Paul warns that the one who eats and drinks without examining his life and without recognizing the body of the Lord brings judgment on himself. Because of this, many believers have gotten sick and even died (1 Cor 11:27–32)! Just as a dead man can do nothing, so too, a dead faith does not work. The admonition is to realize a dead faith cannot save a man from judgment. A live faith not only saves you from certain penalties, it is good for others and allows you to inherit treasures.

It is a popular view that we will all throw our rewards at the feet of Jesus. People cite the twenty-four elders who lay down their crowns in Rev 4 (there is a song about this in many churches). There are some interpretive obstacles to identifying all believers with the twenty-four elders and with saying the crowns they lay at the feet of Jesus are *all* the rewards they receive. The primary obstacles are the clear teachings, in other areas of Scripture already mentioned, that say people will receive rewards for what they do.

---

3. Zane Hodges has also produced a lot of work on this subject that I'd recommend. For example, *The Hungry Inherit: Winning the Wealth of the World to Come* is a good book that discusses eternal rewards.

LOVE STORY FROM THE BATTLEFIELD

If there is no difference between the rewarded and unrewarded believers, then why make such a big deal about the believer who escapes as through a fire as he is no different from any other believer? Of course, they may say that guy has nothing to offer at Jesus's feet and the others do. It seems more plausible, given the text of Rev 20:12, that all will be judged according to what they have done.

This can be very inspiring for many believers and can motivate to action. We are admonished by our Lord to seek first God's kingdom and righteousness, along with storing up for ourselves treasures in heaven (Matt 6). For believers, this means there will be different rewards in heaven based on faithfulness. For unbelievers, it means there will be different punishments in hell based on how they acted as well. This resonates with the divine attribute of God's justice—giving each person what they rightly deserve.

As we continue our study of the word of God, let us realize that the Bible is a love story and we are on a battlefield for the hearts of mankind. There are spiritual forces of darkness that are our primary enemies, and God has given us all we need to stand against them (Eph 6:10–18). Each idea gleaned from the Scripture has consequences for how we act. Therefore, "let us throw off everything that hinders and the sin that so easily entangles, and let us run with perseverance the race marked out for us. Let us fix our eyes on Jesus, the author and perfecter of our faith. For the joy set before him he endured the cross, scorning its shame, and sat down at the right hand of the throne of God. Consider him who endured such opposition from sinners, so that you will not grow weary and lose heart" (Heb 12:1–3).

9

PUTTING ON THE BULLETPROOF VEST

THE INERRANCY DEBATE

Parents have to decide when to start telling their children about different evils in the world. Our responsibility is not only to disabuse our children of thinking about monsters under the bed, but to equip them to realize the dangers of moving vehicles. Just as the basics of teaching a child to look both ways before crossing the street are important for a child's well-being, so too understanding how to interpret the Bible is necessary for Christian growth.

In the course of this book we've discussed many areas related to the Scripture to help strengthen your faith. One of the best ways to increase our understanding is to read the works of those who have studied the Scriptures deeply. Just like in different churches, there are scholars who don't share all of our same theological views. Nevertheless, reading a broad number of people gives us insight into elements of the text that we may have never considered. This instruction from others is very valuable to allow us to discover the context of the Scripture. However, in the course of study, one danger is that some scholars don't believe the Bible is without error.

PUTTING ON THE BULLETPROOF VEST

In the recent history of American Protestantism there has been a debate about inerrancy (whether the Bible is without error in the original manuscripts). There are many people who love God, defend Christianity broadly speaking, and can teach many about new ways to understand the Scripture while holding that there are certain mistakes in the Bible. Just as it is important to teach our kids to avoid physical dangers, so too it is good for Christians to be informed of the basics about the inerrancy debate and a general way to approach it.

Some hold to a view that the Scripture has no errors in matters of faith and practice, but in matters of science and history there are minor errors. The claim is that the Bible tells you how to go to heaven and not how the heavens go. This chapter will survey this debate, provide some resources, and direct those interested in inerrancy for deeper study.

WHY IS THIS IMPORTANT?

There are some who argue that defending inerrancy is not important. For example, the great preacher Charles Haddon Spurgeon said,

> There seems to me to have been twice as much done in some ages in defending the Bible as in expounding it, but if the whole of our strength shall henceforth go to the exposition and spreading of it, we may leave it pretty much to defend itself. I do not know whether you see that lion—it is very distinctly before my eyes; a number of persons advance to attack him, while a host of us would defend the grand old monarch, the British Lion, with all our strength. Many suggestions are made and much advice is offered. This weapon is recommended, and the other. Pardon me if I offer a quiet suggestion. Open the door and let the lion out; he will take care of himself. Why, they are gone! He no sooner goes forth in his strength than his assailants flee. The way to meet

infidelity is to spread the Bible. The answer to every objection against the Bible is the Bible.[1]

The analogy Spurgeon uses here is to compare Scripture with a lion that can do more than take care of itself. However, as the inerrancy of Scripture is under attack, one response to Spurgeon's view is the biblical admonition to "demolish arguments and every thought that sets itself against the knowledge of God" (2 Cor 10:5).

There are a number of reasons that can be given as to why the inerrancy of Scripture is so important. Jesus himself indicates the importance of inerrancy when he speaks with Nicodemus. Think about what Jesus says in John 3:12: "I have spoken to you of earthly things and you do not believe; how then will you believe if I speak of heavenly things?" Note that Nicodemus is rebuked for not believing in things that he can verify. If people can't believe aspects of the Bible that can be checked out, Jesus seems to indicate this will impact their faith in things that can't be confirmed (e.g., truths of the faith like the Trinity, the substitutionary atonement, and the dual natures of Christ). In other words, Nicodemus can check out parts of what Jesus was saying and not believe it. Why would he, or anyone for that matter, ever believe aspects that simply have to be taken by faith?

Some truths of the faith are knowable by reason. Truths knowable by reason can be discovered through historical investigation or philosophy. For example, one can reason to the fact that God exists. Similarly, people can verify that Israelites were once slaves in Egypt. Even though you can discover these truths in ways that are outside the Bible, one can certainly know these truths just from reading the Bible as well (since the Bible is a historical document). These are truths of reason.

Other Christian doctrines can only be known because God has revealed it to us by His word. These would be the things previously mentioned. One does not ascertain the substitutionary atonement in a science lab. It would be impossible for these types of truths to be known in this way as this subject matter is beyond the realm of

---

1. Spurgeon, *Speeches at Home and Abroad*, 14.

PUTTING ON THE BULLETPROOF VEST

what science can measure. The method by which you study some things excludes things that fall outside the method. All this simply means is that we have certain methods that only describe part of reality. For example, one can see that placing a metal detector within a doorway may be able to tell you whether a person carries a metal weapon through the door. It does *not* include the fact there may still be weapons that are *not metal* passing through the door (e.g., Chuck Norris or David's mighty warriors in 2 Sam 23:8–39). This is simply an illustration describing the fact that certain aspects of reality are known in different ways. Some things about reality are known by faith because God has told us and some are known using other ways the Lord has provided.

The debate about whether there are errors in the Bible is really hundreds of years old. Answers for the critics of the Bible have been around just as long. The most complete statement about biblical inerrancy has been expounded in the Chicago Statement on Biblical Inerrancy (CSBI). The statement grew out of the International Conference on Biblical Inerrancy (ICBI), an event in October of 1978 that had more than three hundred Christian scholars, leaders, and pastors, who met to describe fully the doctrine of inerrancy.[2] Regarding the importance of inerrancy, Norman Geisler explains,

1. It is attached to the character of God,
2. It is foundational to other essential doctrines,
3. It is taught in the Scriptures, and
4. It is the historic position of the Christian Church.[3]

Each of these would alone be sufficient to pay attention to the doctrine of inerrancy. Together, they should make us take notice of the debate, which is still influencing many today.

---

2. http://library.dts.edu/Pages/TL/Special/ICBI.shtml
3. Geisler, "Review of 'Five Views on Biblical Inerrancy,'" 30.

Reading to Grow

WHAT IS THE DEBATE?

In studying the inerrancy debate there are two major areas of contention. First, both those in support of and those against inerrancy argue about how to define this term. The definition of inerrancy in this case is important to discover who holds this doctrine according to a particular definition. Second, there is a debate about the methodological approach one uses when dealing with the topic of errors in the Bible. This asks what the method is when thinking about an error in Scripture.

As for the definition of inerrancy, there are a range of contrary views. Although broadly understood to mean the Bible has no errors in what it affirms, the debate goes into what is actually affirmed. When people discuss the subject, try to glean which definition they mean when using the word inerrancy. The three major options for inerrancy are explained by Millard J. Erickson.

1. **Full Inerrancy** is the view that the Bible is completely truthful in all that it teaches, but that not all of its allusions need be regarded as assertions.

2. **Limited Inerrancy** is a reference to the belief that the inerrancy of the Bible is limited in some way. A common version says that the Bible is inerrant in its theological or salvific references, but not in its references to matters of history and science.

3. **Inerrancy of Purpose** is the view that the Scripture will not fail to accomplish its purposes, even if factual errors are involved at some point.[4]

Those who drafted the CSBI define inerrancy in terms of unlimited inerrancy, which affirms the Bible is true about everything it addresses—"whether it is redemption, ethics, history, science, or anything else."[5] Full inerrancy and unlimited inerrancy are the same in this description.

---

4. Erickson, *Concise Dictionary of Christian Theology*, 82–83.
5. Geisler, "Review of 'Five Views on Biblical Inerrancy,'" 29.

What is it that one has to assume or presuppose when discussing inerrancy? It seems that one has to know the difference between the truth and an error. The definition of truth and error are not only embedded in any talk of inerrancy, but ought to be part of the explicit discussion. The reason this is important is because people believe different definitions of truth. Some say that truth is what works (it is pragmatic). In other words, if something works it is true; if it doesn't it is false. Others believe truth is something that is internally consistent (or coherent). This says if a story you tell is self-consistent then it is true. Another group says truth is what corresponds to reality. In this view, if you say something is the case and what you said matches what actually happened—it is true. It should be made clear up front that a person's definition of truth is a part of the discussion on inerrancy.

It will not do to pretend there is an agreement when there is not due to a misunderstanding at a more foundational level. So, even if two people say they hold to full inerrancy as Erickson describes, but they disagree about the definition of truth, they still won't hold to the same view of inerrancy. For example, suppose both claim to believe in full inerrancy but one says truth is only what works and another that it is what is internally consistent. If the statement in Scripture works to bring someone to the faith, then the pragmatist would say it is true (even if the statement doesn't match reality). If a statement in Scripture is consistent to all the other verses, it would be true (whether or not the claim every really happened). This just touches on the differences. We will return to a correct definition of truth shortly.

WHO ARE THE MAJOR THINKERS?

An instructor should equip people with the best thinkers in a debate on the subject he is teaching. The major thinkers that hold to a different view on inerrancy help us sift the wheat from the chaff. Yet some object to identifying those with the wrong view of inerrancy. Yet consider that we know the names of the apostles. It was also important to them that we all know the names of those who have the wrong views on different subjects. Consider the biblical example of "naming names."

There is justification in the Bible to identify false teachers (which is the example set by the apostles) in 2 Tim 1:13-18 and 2 Tim 4:14, among other places. The church is warned about Phygellus, Hermogenes, Philetus, Jannes, Jambres, Demas, and Alexander the coppersmith, as well as others. Thus, it is good to know some of the leaders in both camps (both those who defend and reject inerrancy).

Although there are more that can be listed, here are some that affirm unlimited inerrancy. Some of those who were part of the executive council of ICBI in 1978 were Gleason L. Archer, James M. Boice, Edmund P. Clowney, Norman L. Geisler, John H. Gerstner, Harold W. Hoehner, Kenneth Kantzer, James I. Packer, Francis A Schaeffer, and R. C. Sproul. More recent defenders of this view include Thomas A. Howe, F. David Farnell, William C. Roach, Richard G. Howe, William E. Nix, and Albert Mohler. For the more recent defenders, you can find their writings on this subject without much difficulty online.

At the time of the publication of this text, the modern leaders that reject the ICBI statement of inerrancy are Michael Bird, Peter Enns, Kevin Vanhoozer, John Franke, Michael Licona, Robert Gundry, and Craig Blomberg. Those who were influential in the 1960s were Daniel Fuller, George Ladd, Paul Jewett, Jack Rogers, and the president of Fuller Seminary, David Hubbard. In addition, before the ICBI statement was framed, there have been other influential thinkers who have attacked the biblical text (some Christian and some not). Here are some:

1. Julius Wellhausen popularized the view that Moses didn't write the Pentateuch, but it is the work of four authors—this is called the JEPD theory or the Documentary Hypothesis.

2. Rudolph Bultmann developed an approach to Scripture that removed anything that appears to be miraculous, saying these are myth and not history.

PUTTING ON THE BULLETPROOF VEST

3. Karl Barth is the father of Neo-Orthodoxy, and claims that the Bible is a "witness to the Word of God." Note that this differs from saying the Bible *is* the word of God.

4. Dietrich Bonhoeffer held the Bible is historically unreliable and filled with errors based on myths.[6]

5. C. S. Lewis also can be considered as a Neo-Evangelical as he defended certain tenets of Christianity, but rejected inerrancy. He accepted there are certain historical errors (like the story of Jonah) which, in his opinion, do not exclude the truth of Christianity.[7]

HOW CAN WE NAVIGATE THE WATERS ON INERRANCY?

The chapter titled "The Basics of Biblical Interpretation" discussed how to deal with Bible difficulties. Remember that the most important principle in interpretation is context. In this section, realize the importance and potential dangers of philosophy for interpretation. One truth gleaned from the course of my studies at seminary was that the greatest theological dangers Christians face comes from bad philosophy. Bad philosophy is such that it undermines certain aspects of Christianity and is best countered by good philosophy. Philosophy as a discipline affects our interpretation in that it deals not only with how things are defined (like truth), but also questions like what is reality, how do we know things, and where is meaning found. These are all important issues that a person has answers to before coming to the biblical text.

Of course, it is easy to see how this is important in the realm where one has learned to defend the faith (a course or book of the basics of apologetics—which is the art of giving a reason for

---

6. See Weikart, *Myth of Dietrich Bonhoeffer*; Weikart, "So Many Different Dietrich Bonhoeffers"; and Weikart, "Scripture and Myth in Dietrich Bonhoeffer." These articles are available at www.csustan.edu/history/faculty/weikart.

7. An individual can find a full explanation of these historical figures along with a response to their positions in Geisler, *Systematic Theology*, 315–408.

Christianity—can help here). When one is doing apologetics, the individual presents reasons to believe in God's existence, why certain events should be recognized as miracles, or how we can know certain truths (like that Jesus rose from the dead).

In another related realm, it doesn't take much to see how philosophy is useful for polemics (i.e., defending certain aspects of orthodoxy from within the church). Take the issue of truth that was previously mentioned. What is the source definition of "truth?" "Truth" can be one of the following:

1. The correspondence or identity between what is said and what is real.
2. The pragmatic view says truth is what works. That is to say, if something works, then it is true.
3. The coherence view says that truth is something that holds together and doesn't contradict itself.
4. The intentional theory says that we need to look at the author's intentions and not whether the statement matches reality.

The problem with definitions 2–4 is that they are inadequate views of truth.

For the pragmatic view described in definition 2, I can tell a lie that may work, but that wouldn't make my lie true. Or, suppose my children ask about why I go to the gas station. I go on to explain that I have to feed my chipmunks and that this what the gas pump does. You see, I tell them, my car is run by chipmunks that live under the hood and as long as I feed them, the car runs. As my car keeps running (namely, it works), if the pragmatic view is correct, then so is my explanation. However, my explanation is clearly false!

Similarly, a problem with definition 3 is that one can tell a story that is completely coherent and it may still not be true. Consider all the fictional stories that have no contradictions (e.g., Tolkien's *The Lord of the Rings*). Does that make these stories true? By no means. Thus, because fictional stories are not true just because they are without contradiction, so too the coherence view is not an adequate theory of truth.

Those promoting the intentional view described in number 4 ask us to redefine how we normally understand truth and error. This theory says that one only need to examine whether the intention is wrong or not. This view would be in accord with what Erickson has called "inerrancy of purpose." The theory shifts the burden for truth and falsity away from whether a statement is true and places it solely in the author's mind. If an author didn't intend to deceive or say something false, we shouldn't judge it that way. For example, William Lane Craig uses an example to defend an intentional view by discussing Jesus's reference to the mustard seed being the smallest of seeds (because it is not actually the smallest seed in the entire world).[8] He claims that we judge the intention of his story and not the claim.[9] If Jesus's intention is simply to illustrate another point, then his claim shouldn't be judged. However, we all know that good or bad intentions are different from the truth of statements. It's not proper to conflate the two areas. I may be sincere and have the best intentions of telling someone that I have lots of money in the bank accessible to pay my bills. However, if unbeknownst to me the government has frozen my accounts for some reason then—regardless of my intentions—my statement is not true. This view fails to take into account the plain way we all speak of claims being true or false.

Does the correspondence theory face similar problems? Fortunately, it does not. The correspondence theory, which states that what is said corresponds to reality, is at the foundation of every other theory. Truth as correspondence is foundational and you can tell it is so just by reflecting upon our speech or writing. Consider the word "is" and the role it plays. When I say, "A girl is leaving the store," the "is" in the statement is significant. It affirms something about reality. If a girl really is doing what the statement says, you

---

8. Incidentally, the verse does not illustrate an error that Jesus made once the context is understood. Jesus was addressing a first-century Israeli farmer and this was the smallest of seeds that he would sow in his field.

9. Geisler, "Biblical Inerrancy, Inductive or Deductive Basis," 134

know it is true. This is because what is said corresponds to reality. Note also how the pragmatic and coherence view both use the word "is" as an aspect of their description (e.g., truth is what works or truth is what does not contradict). Other theories can't avoid using the correspondence view in their rejection of correspondence. The correspondence view is foundationally undeniable (for to deny it would use it). Keep your eyes open for the word "is," which supports the correspondence theory. For example, the critic says, "The correspondence theory *is* not the correct theory of truth." The "is" in this criticism is an embedded correspondence view that refers to the statement's correspondence (or identity) to reality in order to deny that a statement's truth is its correspondence to reality. This is clearly contradictory.

The Council on Biblical Inerrancy affirms the correspondence view. It also explicitly rejects several of the other views that were mentioned. This is found in both the statement on inerrancy and on hermeneutics. In the ICBI statement, Article XIII on inerrancy says,

> We deny that it is proper to evaluate Scripture according to standards of truth and error that are alien to its usage or purpose. We further deny that inerrancy is negated by biblical phenomena such as a lack of modern technical precision, irregularities of grammar or spelling, observational descriptions of nature, the reporting of falsehoods [e.g., Satan's lie], the use of hyperbole and round numbers, the topical arrangement of the material, variant selections of material in parallel account, or the use of free citations.[10]

Article VI of the Chicago Statement of Biblical Hermeneutics is the clearest expression of the explicit affirmation of a correspondence view.

> We affirm that the Bible expresses God's truth in propositional statements, and we declare that biblical truth is both objective and absolute. We further affirm that a statement is true if it represents matters as they actually

---

10 The original document is in the Dallas Theological Seminary Archives. As of December 16, 2016, you can also access it here: http://library.dts.edu/Pages/TL/Special/ICBI_1.pdf.

PUTTING ON THE BULLETPROOF VEST

are, but is an error if it misrepresents the facts. We deny that, while Scripture is able to make us wise unto salvation, biblical truth should be defined in terms of this function. We further deny that error should be defined as that which willfully deceives.[11]

My encouragement is for those who are interested in this subject to do two things. First, read the statements from the ICBI. These are very short and yet very explanatory. They can provide tools to understand nuances within the debate and how we interpret the Bible. Second, become acquainted with the resources provided on the defending inerrancy website.[12] There are scholars on this site that respond to the latest attacks on the trustworthiness of the Bible.

Recall the syllogism mentioned in "The Basics of Biblical Interpretation" for inerrancy:

1. The Bible teaches God cannot error, and
2. The Bible is the Word of God.
3. From these two it follows logically and necessarily that the Bible cannot error.

This syllogism rests on what is called deductive logic. Premises 1 and 2 we are able to glean from reading the text. The reasoning we use to discern these things is inductive. Based on the laws of thought—which are gleaned from reality—one must agree with the logical conclusion that follows from the deductive syllogism. To reject inerrancy one must either say God can error or that the Bible is not the word of God. If one affirms both points 1 and 2, then inerrancy follows.

There are a host of other reasons that can also be given for inerrancy. Here are four short reasons to remember when discussing whether the Scripture has errors.

---

11. Here is a link for the Chicago Statement of Biblical Hermeneutics as of December 16, 2016: http://library.dts.edu/Pages/TL/Special/ICBI_2.pdf.

12. As of December 16, 2016, this site provides resources for defending inerrancy: http://defendinginerrancy.com/.

1. God affirms His word is true and inerrant in the Old Testament and in the New Testament (Ps 119:160; John 10:35).

2. The nature of God ensures inerrancy. God is truth and cannot error; He promises His word will never pass away even if all else does; and God has the strength to ensure it never passes away. If Scripture is corrupt or in error, this undermines the attributes of God.

3. Inerrancy is the consistent position of the Bible, the church fathers, the medieval theologians, the reformers, and leaders of the church throughout all of church history until relatively recently.

4. None of the alleged "errors" that biblical critics bring up actually need to be interpreted as mistakes in the text. There is "a lack of proven error."

Thus, given the syllogism and corroboration of all these points, one has a powerful case for inerrancy upon which we can rest.

Keep in mind the admonition to be wise as serpents and innocent as doves. Wisdom tells us that some truths come from the mouth of those who don't believe entirely as we do. C. S. Lewis aptly said,

> To be ignorant and simple now—not to be able to meet the enemies on their own ground—would be to throw down our weapons, and to betray our uneducated brethren who have, under God, no defense but us against the intellectual attacks of the heathen. Good philosophy must exist, if for no other reason, because bad philosophy needs to be answered. The cool intellect must work not only against cool intellect on the other side, but against the muddy heathen mysticisms which deny intellect altogether.[13]

The goal of loving God with all our mind means we should know Him through His word. Defending inerrancy and studying the context of Scripture aids us to this end and has practical

---

13. Lewis, "Learning in War-Time."

ramifications because beliefs have consequences. The finger of God on all of Scripture should motivate us to understand and wield the Word properly. Remember that "the word of God is living and active, sharper than any double-edged sword, penetrating even to dividing soul and spirit, joint and marrow, judging the thoughts and attitudes of the heart" (Heb 4:12). What good would it be for any of us to gain the whole world and lose our soul (Mark 8:36)?

It is important to note that those on both sides of the current inerrancy debate will agree to the following for a rich Christian life. Read the Bible to grow in your faith. Be strong in the Lord. Equip yourself with the full armor of God. Pray always. Immerse yourself in the word of God—doing what it says—to stand against the spiritual forces of evil. Love God and each other. Look forward to the heavenly Jerusalem, the city of the living God, which shall never be shaken. Know that our work in God will be rewarded. In accord with Paul's letter to the Ephesians, may "the eyes of your heart be enlightened in order that you may know the hope to which he has called you, the riches of his glorious inheritance in the saints, and his incomparably great power for us who believe" (Eph 1:18–19 NIV).

APPENDIX

GUIDELINES FOR BIBLE STUDY

OBSERVATIONS

Key terms, figures of speech, outline the structure, genre, historical context, author and audience, people involved, location.

1. Note difficulties in the text (ambiguous language or structure, tension with other scripture, etc.).
2. Consult a Bible dictionary for more historical context and look up the different meanings for key or repeated words used in the text. Write your observations based on this.
3. What is the genre of the section and how does it relate to similar books?

INTERPRETATION OF THE MEANING

Grammatical, structural, literary analysis, parallel passages, and theological context.

1. Consult different translations (pay attention to differences in translation). Note these differences.
2. What is the argument of the text (if there is one)?

GUIDELINES FOR BIBLE STUDY

3. Read several commentaries to get different views *after* you've read the passage. Explain what your interpretation is in comparison with other interpretations.

APPLICATION

Do what the text says based on universal principles!

1. What are the universal principles applying to our circumstances?
2. How can I put what I am reading into practice today?
3. What do I need to work on based on the interpretation of the text?
4. Does this give me any instruction as to how to pray?
5. What instruction about God can I glean from this?
6. How can I love others based on what the text says?

Bibliography

Augustine, Saint, Bishop of Hippo. *Confessions.* New York: Penguin, 1961.
Black, David Alan. *New Testament Textual Criticism: A Concise Guide.* Grand Rapids: Baker Books, 1994.
Carson, D. A. *Exegetical Fallacies.* Grand Rapids: Baker Books, 1996.
Clarke, W. Norris. *The One and the Many: A Contemporary Thomistic Metaphysics.* Notre Dame: University of Notre Dame Press, 2001.
Couch, Mal, ed. *An Introduction to Classical Evangelical Hermeneutics: A Guide to the History and Practice of Biblical Interpretation.* Grand Rapids: Kregel, 2000.
Dewey, David. *A User's Guide to Bible Translations: Making the Most of Different Versions.* Downers Grove, IL: InterVarsity, 2004.
Ehrman, Bart D. *Misquoting Jesus: The Story Behind Who Changed the Bible and Why.* San Francisco: HarperSanFrancisco, 2005.
Erickson, Millard J. *A Basic Guide to Eschatology: Making Sense of the Millennium.* Grand Rapids: Baker Books, 1998.
———. *Concise Dictionary of Christian Theology.* Grand Rapids: Baker Books, 1994.
Fee, Gordon D., and Douglas Stuart. *How to Read the Bible for All Its Worth.* Grand Rapids: Zondervan, 2003.
Fee, Gordon D., and Mark L. Strauss. *How to Choose a Translation for All Its Worth: A Guide to Understanding and Using Bible Versions.* Grand Rapids: Zondervan, 2007.
Friesen, Garry, and Robin Maxson. *Decision Making and the Will of God.* Colorado Springs: Multnomah Books, 2004.
Geisler, Norman L. "Biblical Inerrancy, Inductive or Deductive Basis: A Response to William Lane Craig." In *Vital Issues in the Inerrancy Debate*, edited by F. David Farnell, 132–44. Eugene, OR: Wipf & Stock, 2015.
———. "A Review of 'Five Views on Biblical Inerrancy.'" In *The Jesus Quest: The Danger from Within*, edited by Norman L. Geisler and F. David Farnell, 28–62. Maitland, FL: Xulon, 2014.
———. *Systematic Theology: In One Volume.* Bloomington, MN: Bethany House, 2011.

BIBLIOGRAPHY

Geisler, Norman L., and Thomas A. Howe. *When Critics Ask: A Popular Handbook on Bible Difficulties.* Grand Rapids: Baker Books, 1992.

Geisler, Norman L., Wayne House, and Max Herrera. *The Battle for God: Responding to the Challenge of Neotheism.* Grand Rapids: Kregel, 2001.

Gilley, Gary. *"I Just Wanted More Land" - Jabez: A Careful Analysis of Bruce Wilkinson's "The Prayer of Jabez."* Maitland, FL: Xulon, 2001.

Greidanus, Sidney. *The Modern Preacher and the Ancient Text: Interpreting and Preaching Biblical Literature.* Grand Rapids: InterVarsity, 1988.

Grudem, Wayne, and Jerry Thacker. *Why Is My Choice of a Bible Translation So Important?* Louisville: Council on Biblical Manhood and Womanhood, 2005.

Hanegraaff, Hank. *The Apocalypse Code: Find Out What the Bible Really Says About the End Times and Why It Matters Today.* Nashville: Thomas Nelson, 2007.

Herrera, Max. "Using Analogies to Reach the Lost and Refute the Cults." *Christian Research Journal* 28 (2005) 10–11.

Hodges, Zane. *Grace in Eclipse: A Study of Eternal Rewards.* Denton, TX: Grace Evangelical Society, 2016.

Howe, Thomas A. "Does Genre Determine Meaning?" In *The Jesus Quest: The Danger from Within*, edited by Norman L. Geisler and F. David Farnell, 523–38. Maitland, FL: Xulon Press, 2014.

———. *Objectivity in Biblical Interpretation.* Altamonte Springs, FL: Advantage Books, 2004.

Hume, David. *The Empiricists.* Garden City, NY: Anchor, 1974.

Kaiser, Walter C., and Moises Silva. *An Introduction to Biblical Hermeneutics: The Search for Meaning.* Grand Rapids: Zondervan, 1994.

Kenyon, Frederic G. *The Bible and Archeology.* New York: Harper, 1940.

Koren, Henry. *An Introduction to the Science of Metaphysics.* St. Louis: B. Herder, 1964.

Kostenberger, Andreas, Darrell Bock, and Josh Chatraw. *Truth Matters: Confident Faith in a Confusing World.* Nashville: B & H, 2014.

Koukl, Gregory. *Never Read A Bible Verse.* Signal Hill, CA: Stand to Reason, 2000.

Kreeft, Peter. *Socratic Logic: A Logic Text Using Socratic Method, Platonic Questions, and Aristotelian Principles.* Edited by Trent Dougherty. South Bend, IN: St. Augustine's, 2005.

Lewis, C. S. "Learning in War-Time." Sermon Preached in the Church of St. Mary the Virgin, Oxford, 1939.

Lightner, Robert P. *The Last Days Handbook: A Comprehensive Guide to Understanding the Different Views of Prophecy, Who Believes What About Prophecy and Why.* Nashville: T. Nelson, 1990.

Martin, John Bartlow. *Adlai Stevenson and The World: The Life of Adlai E. Stevenson.* Garden City, NY: Doubleday, 1977.

Metzger, Bruce, ed. *Chapters in the History of New Testament Textual Criticism.* Grand Rapids: Eerdmans, 1963.

Mondin, Battista. *The Principle of Analogy in Protestant and Catholic Theology.* The Hague: M. Nijhoff, 1963.

BIBLIOGRAPHY

Moody, D. L. *The Overcoming Life*. Chicago: Moody Bible Institute, 1994.

Osborne, Grant R. *The Hermeneutical Spiral: A Comprehensive Introduction to Biblical Interpretation*. Downers Grove, IL: InterVarsity, 1991.

Pearcey, Nancy R. *Saving Leonardo: A Call to Resist the Secular Assault on Mind, Morals, and Meaning*. Nashville: B & H, 2010.

———. *Total Truth: Liberating Christianity from Its Cultural Captivity*. Wheaton, IL: Crossway, 2005.

Peterson, Eugene. *The Message/Remix: The Bible in Contemporary Language*. Colorado Springs: NavPress, 2006.

Ramm, Bernard. *Protestant Biblical Interpretation: A Textbook of Hermeneutics*. 3rd rev. ed. Grand Rapids: Baker Books, 1970.

Rhodes, Ron. *The Complete Guide to Bible Translations*. Eugene, OR: Harvest House, 2009.

Richards, Larry. *735 Baffling Bible Questions Answered*. Grand Rapids: Revell, 1993.

Rinne, Jeramie. *How Will the World End? And Other Questions About the Last Things and the Second Coming of Christ*. Croydon, England: Good Book, 2014.

Roberts, Mark D. *Can We Trust the Gospels: Investigating the Reliability of Matthew, Mark, Luke and John*. Wheaton, IL: Crossway, 2006.

Robinson, John A. T. *An Introduction to the Textual Criticism of the New Testament*. Reprint, Eugene, OR: Wipf & Stock, 1928.

Ryken, Leland. *How to Read the Bible as Literature . . . and Get More Out of It*. Grand Rapids: Zondervan, 1984.

Ryrie, Charles. *Dispensationalism*. Chicago: Moody Press, 1995.

Sire, James. *The Universe Next Door: A Basic Worldview Catalog*. Downers Grove, IL: InterVarsity, 1997.

Sirico, Robert. *Defending the Free Market: The Moral Case for a Free Economy*. New York: Regnery, 2012.

Spurgeon, Charles. *Speeches at Home and Abroad*. Charleston, SC: BiblioBazaar, 1878.

———. *Spurgeon on Prayer and Spiritual Warfare: Satan Considers the Saints*. New Kensington, PA: Whitaker House, 1998.

Strobel, Lee. *The Case for the Real Jesus: A Journalist Investigates Current Attacks on the Identity of Christ*. Grand Rapids: Zondervan, 2007.

Wallace, J. Warner. *Cold Case Christianity: A Homicide Detective Investigates the Claims of the Gospels*. Colorado Springs: David C. Cook, 2013.

Weikart, Richard. *The Myth of Dietrich Bonhoeffer: Is His Theology Evangelical?* San Francisco: International Scholars, 1997.

Weikart, Richard. "Scripture and Myth in Dietrich Bonhoeffer." *Fides et Historia* 25 (1993) 12–25.

———. "So Many Different Dietrich Bonhoeffers." *Trinity Journal* 32 (2011) 69–81.

Wenham, Gordon. *Word Biblical Commentary*. Vol. 1, *Genesis 1–15*. Waco, TX: Word Books, 1987.

www.ingramcontent.com/pod-product-compliance
Lightning Source LLC
Chambersburg PA
CBHW070934160426
43193CB00011B/1687